In Search of Understanding

In Search of Understanding

*Reflections on Christian Engagement with Muslims
after Four Decades of Encounter*

by **Clinton Bennett**

Foreword by Ataullah Siddiqui

WIPF & STOCK · Eugene, Oregon

IN SEARCH OF UNDERSTANDING
Reflections on Christian Engagement with Muslims after Four Decades of Encounter

Copyright © 2019 Clinton Bennett. All rights reserved. Except for brief quotations in critical publications or reviews, no part of this book may be reproduced in any manner without prior written permission from the publisher. Write: Permissions, Wipf and Stock Publishers, 199 W. 8th Ave., Suite 3, Eugene, OR 97401.

Wipf & Stock
An Imprint of Wipf and Stock Publishers
199 W. 8th Ave., Suite 3
Eugene, OR 97401

www.wipfandstock.com

PAPERBACK ISBN: 978-1-5326-4655-3
HARDCOVER ISBN: 978-1-5326-4656-0
EBOOK ISBN: 978-1-5326-4657-7

Manufactured in the U.S.A. OCTOBER 1, 2019

Contents

Foreword by Ataullah Siddiqui | vii

Acknowledgments | xi

Introduction   My Personal Journey | xiii

Chapter One   Can Christians Appreciate the Prophet Muhammad as a Genuine Messenger from God or Is This Theological Treason? | 1

Chapter Two   How Might Christians Respond to the Muslim Claim That Jesus Was a Prophet and Is Not God Incarnate? | 26

Chapter Three   Can Christians with Integrity Regard the Qurʾān as a Word from God? | 45

Chapter Four   Is There Any Possibility of Rapprochement on the Issue of Whether Jesus Died on the Cross? | 60

Chapter Five   The State of Official Church-Related Christian-Muslim Dialogue | 73

Chapter Six   Suggestions on How Christians Can Challenge Negative Tropes about Muslims and Cooperate in Peace and Justice Advocacy, Social and Community Development | 83

Conclusion | 106

Bibliography | 109

General Index | 117

Scripture Index | 123

Foreword

THE Christian-Muslim relationship is a hyphenated connection; close and yet retaining elements of detachment. Despite fundamental differences in creed, Muslims remain honorable to Mary and Jesus and they furnish a significant part of their faith. Special status is also accorded to Christians as the "people of the book." Christians also hold a central place in Islam's theological cosmology. Belief may have been a serious contender for the separation of creed but I believe that "history" and "memory" create that hyphen, as a negative force firmly between the two. "History" is not a neutral entity and "memory" is selective.

Clinton Bennett has been preoccupied over the years with both the differences and the commonality in Christian-Muslim relations. He has skillfully examined such history in his books *Victorian Images of Islam* and *Understanding Christian-Muslim Relations*. He has further analyzed postwar rethinking among Christians about their relationship with other faith communities, especially with Muslims. He, in some ways, tries to optimally promote the relationship.

The significant progress made by the declarations of *Nostra Aetete* and the *Guidelines* that were provided by the Vatican and the World Council of Churches, respectively, to their members, helped in building confidence and trust. Bennett successfully explores such development and its impact throughout his writings. He is a keen student of past relations and a serious observer of contemporary engagement between the two communities. In addition to his role within the British Council of Churches, which he helped to restructure while he was in England, he is directly involved in a bilateral initiative of the National Muslim Christian Initiative (NMCI) in the United States. The organization that emerged in the wake of 9/11 and the "Common Word" initiative are examples of Christians and Muslims seeking a way forward together. Increasingly, the conditions in which such confidence-building initiatives are considered face serious challenges. Sociopolitical conditions, the uncertain economic climate and, above all, the

FOREWORD

age of social media have contributed toward generating mistrust, observing people engaging in vicious polemics. I am not denying social media as a potential force for good, despite its less constructive elements. In some respects, it provides an opportunity to resurrect past polemics, strip away the context and apply it in a very simplified and distorted manner. In a state of such upheaval, subjects such as Christian-Muslim relations, particularly within the current climate, command our full attention.

It is always difficult to find a person who has experience working among Christians and Muslims at the grassroots level—teaching, learning, and engaging with people's concerns; while involved in academic study of the subject by critiquing, reflecting, and exploring new avenues of enquiry. Bennett's strength is that he "glides with ease" and engages with confidence during a career that reflects his involvement. In this book—a text that largely reflects on the past activities of the author's work—his qualities manifest. He discusses his experiences working with Muslims, while living and learning among them. He has worked in Asia, Australia, Europe, and America with various levels of responsibility. He reflects on his roles having helped shape and guide the two communities' relationships so mired in past memories. Memories that are vested in perceptions and misperceptions; they are shaped by past conflicts and concordances, and such memories switch between dialogue and diatribe depending on the sociopolitical climate of the time. The impacts of such past relations are still actively present among us. Against such a backdrop, Bennett examines his relationship with his own church and other churches.

Bennett's treatment of the subject is never dull and is always rewarding. His handling of the issues central to Christian-Muslim relations reveals a reflective mind that is not satisfied with the soporific effects of "relaxed" dialogue. He enquires, investigates, and challenges where necessary, and proposes new avenues in order to explore future relations. He boldly suggests, for example, whether "Muhammad could be an example and model for Christians, especially in the realm of social ethics and social justice."

Bennett has a sympathetic understanding of those Muslims and Christians whose outlooks differ from his own. Muslims believe that Jesus did not die on the cross, and Bennett asserts that various Christian theologians also share this belief. He is continually observing, reflecting, and rediscovering new relationships. This at times puts him at odds with his fellow Christians.

FOREWORD

Over the years, Bennett has successfully deployed considerable energy in educating his own and other communities to value engagement and dialogue. Through his teaching in universities or in field engagements, he has been true to his conviction that dialogue—and not diatribe—is the way forward for better relations and understanding.

Bennett always learns from his experiences and engages with Muslims in their understanding of relations, based on their basic beliefs and practices. This book draws upon those experiences and reflects his own traditions with Muslims and encourages all to "redraw the map" of Christian-Muslim relations. He argues that relations should not be over-imposing nor gravitate in one direction but should be dual-tracked, multifocal, and multilayered.

In some ways, this book is not about dialogue between two communities; it presents a voice of someone who has experienced and internalized dialogue. In the book, a dialogue partner is not present (and is not meant to be); it is a self-reflective exposition covering forty years. It describes the learning acquired from engagement and suggests changes.

Looking at the relations between the two communities, there is no "universal norm" to be applied wherever required. Relations between the two cannot be managed from a single approach; rather, it requires a multifocused one. Various geographical regions, such as the Far East, South Asia, and North and Southern Africa, or the issues and challenges posed by migrant communities in Europe and in North America, are at different stages of engagement, but each is shaped by the past and each carries its own memories. We are, in reality, living in a "hyphenated" coexistence. Bennett raises questions in this book, and in his other publications, from the theological to basic daily encounters in the two communities. He reflects and recounts that if we remain shackled by history and engulfed in our memories, where it will lead us? Bennett is telling us not to be complacent but vigilant.

Ataullah Siddiqui

Acknowledgments

THIS book draws on, revises, and updates some of my previous writing. It aims to locate my thinking on Islam and on Christian-Muslim relations in the context of my life experience of engagement and encounter. My hope is that this will offer some guidance to others who are involved in or who are thinking about becoming involved in Christian-Muslim relations. The most original chapter, the sixth, though, was almost wholly written for this publication. My introduction refers to many of the thinkers whose work has influenced mine. I openly acknowledge my debt to these scholars and activists without whose contributions I would have little to say. I am also grateful to those publishers and editors of volumes to which I have contributed over the years for the opportunities they provided for me to develop my thinking and ideas on a range of issues. My introduction reworks a recent chapter I wrote for a *festschrift* honoring a former colleague. This is not yet in print so I am unable to give publication details without spoiling the surprise intended for the honoree when it appears. Chapter 1 draws mainly on my contribution to the *Routledge Handbook on Christian Muslim Relations* (2017), "Christians and Muḥammad," and on my chapter, "Christian Perceptions of Muḥammad," in the forthcoming volume *Christian-Muslim Relations: A Thematic History; The First Millennium (600–1600)*, edited by Douglas Pratt and David Thomas, due during 2019. Chapter 2 builds on my contribution to *Jesus and the Incarnation: Reflections of Christians from Islamic Contexts* (2011), edited by David Emmanuel Singh, "Saints, Incarnation and Christian-Muslim Relations: Reflections inspired by encountering Bangladeshi Islam." Chapter 3 develops material from my *Interpreting the Qur'an: A Guide for the Uninitiated* (2009) and from chapter 4, "Muslim Voices on the Qur'an," of *Muslims and Modernity: Current Debates* (2005). Chapter 4 reprises "A Christian Response to the Absence of the Cross in Islam," in *Jesus and the Cross: Reflections of Christians from Islamic Contexts* (2008), edited by David Emmanuel Singh, which itself compares my thinking on the cross in two of my earlier books, *In Search of Muhammad* (1998) and *In Search of Jesus* (2001). Chapter 5 adapts my chapter, "Christian-Muslim Relations in the USA: A Postmodern Analysis after 9/11," in *Contemporary Muslim-Christian Encounters: Developments, Diversity and Dialogue* (2015), edited by Paul Hedges. Finally, although mainly written for this publication, chapter 6 draws on some earlier material from *Muslims and Modernity* and from my *Bloomsbury Companion to Islamic Studies* (2013).

I am also grateful to the Alliance of Baptists for naming me to the National Council of Churches' Convening Table on Inter-Religious Relations, which carries with it membership of the National Muslim-Christian Initiative, whose meetings have offered me opportunities to forge new friendships with leading Muslims in the United States. I also need to acknowledge encouragement from colleagues, friends, family, and members of my church to complete this book. I suffered a heart attack in August followed by major surgery in September 2019, which interrupted this project. I wish to acknowledge my gratitude to the medical team who took such good care of me, especially my cardiologist, Dr. Ali Hammoud, my surgeon, Dr. Alon Aharon, both of Health Quest, Dr. Alison Philip, my primary care physician, and all the nursing and technical staff at Golden Hill Nursing and Rehabilitation Center, where I underwent physical and occupational therapy. Finally, I am very grateful to Ataullah Siddiqui, professor of Christian-Muslim Relations and Interfaith Understanding at and former director of the Markfield Institute of Higher Education, Leicestershire, for contributing the foreword to this book. I very much appreciate his willingness to write this, representing at least one Muslim response to my book.

CLINTON BENNETT
Kingston, New York
August 3, 2019

Introduction

My Personal Journey

THIS book reflects on four decades of engagement, as a pastor and theologian, with Islam and Muslims, drawing on earlier writing and on my participation in Christian-Muslim relations and dialogue. This engagement has included missionary service in Bangladesh (1979–1982), work with the Bangladeshi diaspora in Birmingham, UK, visits to Muslim majority Egypt, Indonesia, Malaysia, Morocco, Turkey, and the Palestinian National Territory, academic study and taking part in formal dialogues linked with the World Council of Churches, and, currently, with the National Council of the Churches of Christ USA (NCCC). Since 2014, I have represented the Alliance of Baptists on the NCCC's Convening Table for Interreligious Relations and on the National Muslim-Christian Initiative. I previously served on the staff of the British Council of Churches, where I was responsible for interfaith relations (1987–1992). During the past forty years I have taught at several colleges, shared in pastoral oversight in various capacities, and worked closely with many not-for-profit organizations promoting collaboration between faith communities. What follows explores some of the issues that dominate Christian thinking on Islam, offering my ideas and describing my experiences of encounter. My engagement with Islam can be seen as a quest or search for understanding, which gave me this book's title. Four of my earlier titles begin with "In Search of." This one, which includes autobiographical content, represents an attempt to gather my thoughts into a single volume from a variety of publications as identified in the acknowledgments.

This book perhaps also aims to systematize my thought, even though I should admit that "systematic theology" has never attracted me. I remain suspicious that attempts to produce comprehensive systems of theology covering all fields within a single theoretical framework confuse what is provisional in our thinking with fixed, immutable ideas. A recurring theme in this book is a call to admit that much of what we believe theologically may be true but is not exhaustive of truth, which leaves room for paradox on such issues as whether God is One, or One in Three Persons and on how essential explicit faith in Jesus is for salvation. I like Anselm's definition of theology as "faith seeking understanding," which suggests that our attempt at understanding faith continues throughout life and, who knows, perhaps beyond! Tracing the development of my thinking in the context of my career, this introduction identifies and acknowledges my debt to those who influenced my ideas. However, in four decades I have had the privilege of meeting many of the leading contributors in the field, both scholars and practitioners, making it difficult to do justice to everyone on whose shoulders I stand. Others are identified as I cite their work. Finally, this introduction gives an overview of the rest of the book.

My Initial Engagement with Islam

My engagement with Islam began in September 1978, when, designated for missionary service in Bangladesh, I was sent for orientation and training to the Selly Oak Colleges, Birmingham. Until it ceased operating at the end of the twentieth century this ecumenical federation of small colleges mainly run by Christian mission agencies functioned throughout the twentieth century as a center for missionary education, and as a place where partners in mission from overseas received training in a variety of areas. It shared with the University of Birmingham the UK's sole chair in mission. I was to live for the next year in St Andrew's Hall, a cooperative institute run by the United Reformed Church Mission Department and the Baptist Missionary Society. I was enrolled into a newly launched certificate of professional studies in Islam at the Centre for the Study of Islam and Christian-Muslim Relations, one of the colleges' central programs. The center itself was new (founded 1976) but built on a legacy of studying Islam at Selly Oak that dated from the arrival of Alphonse Mingana (1878–1937), to whom Birmingham owes many of its Arabic manuscripts, in 1913. The course was accredited by the University of Birmingham. The center (known later as CSIC) taught and supervised all the university's postgraduate degrees and diplomas in Islamic studies until it merged with the university in 2000. It was absorbed into the Centre for Middle Eastern and Islamic Studies in 2010. This began a long association with the center, where I later researched

INTRODUCTION—MY PERSONAL JOURNEY

my MA (1983–1985) and my PhD (1985–1989). As I joined the center, I had just completed my ministerial formation at the Northern Baptist College, Manchester, UK. I was ordained July 2, 1978, at Fordhouses Baptist Church, Wolverhampton, which had sent me into ministry. I graduated bachelor of arts in theology from the University of Manchester on July 10, 1978. Early in my studies at Manchester, I became interested in the religions of the Indian subcontinent and chose as many electives in what was then called comparative religion—the United Kingdom's first chair in comparative religion was at Manchester—as the regulations allowed. Partly, liberation theology was so popular at the time that comparative religion presented itself as a field that might distinguish my choice of a theological specialty from that of almost all my peers. Raised in a rural community in New South Wales, Australia (my family migrated there from England, where I was born, in 1966), where religions such as Hinduism and Buddhism were conspicuously absent, I found a great deal to challenge my faith in exploring these traditions that from the beginning also deepened how I understood my faith. My upbringing had depicted these religions as spiritually bankrupt, but as I studied them it became increasingly difficult for me to dismiss them as totally futile, false, or misguided. This led me to question some of the assumptions of my upbringing about the relation between God, religions, and their followers. At this time, theological reflection on these questions was not part of the syllabus at Manchester but I knew that I wanted to pursue this field of enquiry. When I presented myself as a candidate for ordination prior to entering Northern I had assumed that my future would be as pastor of a local Baptist congregation somewhere in Britain. Certainly, the curriculum at Northern Baptist College was almost wholly designed to prepare us for congregational-based ministry. However, when our college principal, Michael H. Taylor, asked me why as a future pastor I was opting for so many courses in comparative religion at a review of my preferences for the following year—I think it was my third year—to my surprise, because I had not given this any thought until then, I found myself replying that I intended to offer myself for missionary service in India. That spur-of-the-moment response set me on the course I have now pursued for the past four decades. During my penultimate year at Northern I was accepted for overseas service by the Baptist Missionary Society (now BMS World Mission). However, they informed me that there were no vacancies in India at the time because visas for missionaries were largely restricted to medical and other non-theology-related personnel. Instead,

I could work in Bangladesh. Although disappointed that this would not take me to India itself (where I have subsequently visited many iconic sites, toured, and taught on summer programs) I was pleased that this would still take me to the subcontinent. Persuaded that missionary service was my vocation at least at that stage in my life I accepted the posting. There was, though, a gap in my preparation; I had not yet read a single book on Islam, and Bangladesh is a Muslim-majority country. When Principal Taylor learned that I would be required to spend a year as a missionary-in-training at the Selly Oak Colleges, skeptical that after four years of ministerial formation this was essential, he enquired about the programs available and recommended that, instead of completing the mission studies course (which would have overlapped considerably with what I had already covered) I enroll in the certificate in the study of Islam. BMS accepted this with the requirement that I did attend some classes in mission studies and those about adjusting to a new culture, especially in a country considered to be part of the so-called developing world. The mission studies program was mainly designed for students with little or no theological or biblical training who would work in such fields as health care or agriculture. My initial interest in exploring the religions of India was, I think, sparked when, traveling back to England from Australia in 1973—intending to spend a year or so in Europe—I visited a temple on the southern tip of Malaysia.

Influences on My Thought

With the center in its third year of life, the academic year 1978 to 1979 was an exciting time to be a student there. The director, David Kerr (1945–2008), was young (only ten years older than myself), dynamic, and visionary. I consider it a high privilege to have been taught and mentored by Kerr, described by Stephen Goodwin, editor of the two-volume tribute to him, as belonging

> to that set of scholars who saw their principle task to be the education, support and development of their *students*; the student subsequently would be the primary witness of the scholar's work, rather than the contemporary tendency, under the pressure of publications-based funding, to issue forth a stream of books.[1]

---

1. Goodwin, *World Christianity*, xv.

Our class included students from Muslim-majority Indonesia, one Muslim convert from Catholicism (who had served as a lay missionary overseas), an Indian from Hyderabad affiliated with the Henry Martyn Institute of Islamic Studies based there, myself, and another Englishman who, like me, was designated to work in a Muslim-majority context. Very soon after our studies began, Professor Syed Hasan Askari (1932–2008), the first Muslim faculty member, joined the center. This was pioneering. At that time, no similar appointment existed at a Christian seminary or mission study institute. There is little doubt that David Kerr, who would supervise my masters and much of my doctoral research, and Hasan Askari, were hugely influential on my thinking, as was my mission studies teacher, Lesslie Newbigin (1909–1998), whose classes were among those I attended. It would be, though, a later book of Newbigin's, *The Gospel in a Pluralist Society* (1989), that made the greatest impact rather than his teaching at Selly Oak.

Those of us who chose Northern Baptist College to train for ministry tended to identify ourselves as liberal or even as radical in terms of a left-right spectrum of theological opinion. We were deeply influenced by two current movements within the Christian world, ecumenism and liturgical renewal, not least of all as represented by the *Taizé* community, which I and most of my peers visited. In Bangladesh, I would spend some time with the Brothers at their outpost in Chittagong (they later moved to Dhaka). Northern was developing as an ecumenical venture. All worship was shared with Methodist students and faculty who lived alongside us in the same building. We also worked closely with the United Reformed and Unitarian Colleges and with a non-residential Anglican ordination program. These formed the Northern Federation for Training in Ministry and, with other institutions, are now based at Martin Luther King House (formerly the NBC building). We were suspect about approaches to the Christian life that stressed doctrinal conformity—or soundness. For us, action or praxis took priority. Although I would describe my upbringing as a Baptist in Australia as conservative evangelical I had shifted to the left in my thinking by the time I applied to enter theological college. Broadly, this was due to the conviction that the church's mission includes working for social justice, the elimination of poverty, and community solidarity against political oppression and economic exploitation, as well as preaching a message of individual salvation. That is, I believed that God wants us to enjoy health and wholeness in this life not only to secure a place in paradise after death. The "social gospel," pioneered by the Baptist theologian Walter Rauschenbusch (1861–1918), and the more recent proponents of liberation theology loomed large in all our thinking. One of my peers would serve for several decades in Central America, inspired by liberation theology. Yet I do not want to alienate readers who identify as evangelical. For me, sharing faith with Muslims and others is our calling as Christians. I know Muslims who have become Christian and Christians who have become Muslim and I respect their decisions to convert. What for me is at issue is not the imperative to evangelize but how we do so. I try, throughout my theological thinking, to root propositions in biblical interpretation.

When I went to CSIC, whatever I then thought about the necessity of faith in Jesus Christ for salvation, I was aware that BMS was sending me to Bangladesh to "win" Muslim souls for Christ! The assumption was that those who do not accept Jesus as personal lord and savior are spiritually lost. At Selly Oak, however, my thinking underwent revision very quickly. David Kerr set out to teach us Qur'ānic Arabic and the foundations of Muslim faith and practice without intruding his personal opinions into the lectures so that we encountered Islam, as nearly as possible, from a Muslim perspective. Hasan Askari was happy for David Kerr to teach these courses because he trusted that David would not distort what he taught with Christian polemic or criticism of Muslim beliefs. He preferred to lead class discussions on spirituality more generally. He also taught a Bible study on John's gospel. Hasan espoused a spiritual humanism that looks beyond labels and external rites to inner experience of the sacred at the human level. Experiencing how David could teach about Islam without showing hostility, and how Hasan could expound the Bible with reverence and deepen my understanding of the text, raised questions that I had to consider. In one of many references to Jesus' Sermon on the Mount, Askari invites Muslims and Christians to read this together, "to read together the Sermon on the Mount, both for Christians and Muslims, is to bear witness to one of the deepest inter-religious involvements known to history." Reading together leads to the realization that "Jesus, like all prophets, is contemporary to all times."[2] For Hasan, the sermon is about "unity and love" and ethical solidarity.[3] David taught us to recite portions of the Qur'ān without ever impugning what we read, and obviously had a love for and appreciation of the book as if God's word could indeed be heard speaking to

2. Askari, *Spiritual Quest*, 90.
3. Askari, *Spiritual Quest*, 80.

INTRODUCTION—MY PERSONAL JOURNEY

us through this non-Christian scripture. He did nothing to detract from the beauty of the Arabic. Many earlier Christians had derided the Qur'ān as repetitive, absurd, clumsy, confused and contradictory lacking any appealing qualities even if only literary. We also visited mosques where we observed Muslim prayer and attended seminars with students and staff at the Islamic Foundation, Leicester. I began to treat the claim by some Christians that God does not respond to or hear Muslim or Jewish prayer with profound suspicion.

Was it possible, I asked myself, to enjoy a genuine relationship with God without explicit faith in Jesus as the one who died on the cross as the substitution for human sin? Could people for whom Jesus is not the Second Person of a Trinity truly know God, who for Christians exists in a Trinity? I began to doubt that I had the right to judge anyone else's relationship with God or lack of one. I saw Hasan, and other Muslims whom I met, as godly women and men whose prayers and acts of devotion were offered sincerely, whose lives arguably displayed all the virtues that I hope others see in mine which I claim to be one of Christian discipleship, to be a Christ-centered life. This questioning, combined with my appreciation of what several Christian thinkers had written about Islam, meant that when I went to Bangladesh I was much less confident that my task was to "win souls" for Christ. When I reached Bangladesh, what I began was more of an open-ended experience of encountering Muslims, listening and learning from them, than a one-way communication of light into darkness, or of truth against falsehood. Yet the insistent question that kept me occupied was: does such an openness somehow betray my Christian faith? This is probably the key question that features throughout the following chapters. Was I going to Bangladesh under false presences, then, expected by my employers to evangelize Muslims but actually embarking on a somewhat different, even self-indulgent, venture? I had not fully rethought the question of explicit faith as necessary for salvation at this stage. Rather, I was perplexed and conflicted on this not least of all because aspects of what Islam and Christianity teach appear to be irreconcilably different. To the degree that this is possible, resolution of this conundrum, or rather a way to live more comfortably with it, did not come until later in my journey. Two authors whose writing assisted me on that journey are Lewis Bevan Jones (1880–1960) and Kenneth Cragg (1913–2012), whose books I discovered at Selly Oak. I was attracted to both because they had served for many years as missionaries among Muslims, remained earnestly Christian, yet did not feel it necessary to reject Islam as totally false or to deny that Muslims can have any relationship with God. Neither rushed to simplistic or easy judgment on Islam but spent their lives wrestling with its theological and existential challenge. I wrote a research paper on Jones during my Selly Oak studies that later became the basis of my MA thesis. My first trip across the border from Bangladesh to India in 1980 was to attend the fiftieth anniversary celebration of the Henry Martyn Institute of Islamic Studies, Hyderabad, which Jones had cofounded and served as first principal (1930–1941). Jones, a second-generation missionary and a fellow Baptist, was deceased (his death saw expressions of appreciation by Muslims for his life), but I later met Bishop Cragg, whose *The Call of the Minaret* (1956) opened up new possibilities in Christian-Muslim encounter. Less concerned with doctrinal disputation, it sees the mutual exploration of spirituality and devotion as areas where Muslims and Christians can find affinity. Cragg saw conceptual convergence as more important than literal or verbal congruence between the two faiths, speaking of what he called "inter-theology." Cragg wrote a chapter on Hasan Askari in *The Pen and the Faith* (1985), commenting that "his reading of the Qur'an suggests lively possibilities of Muslim-Christian kinship and, so doing, central areas of interior questioning for both."[4] I believe that a faith that fails to constantly ask questions about itself is complacent and lifeless. Later, I would also meet another thinker whose work I encountered at Selly Oak, Wilfred Cantwell Smith (1916–2000). We read his *The Meaning and End of Religion* (1963) in seminar. This book did much to shift the focus of my thoughts from what religions claim as truth vis-à-vis their rivalry with other religions to the faith in people's hearts. Smith saw this as distinct from the systems of belief and practice with which people identify. Religions are cumulative constructs; faith is personal piety, awe of the divine, experience of and encounter with the sacred, which for Smith is a human universal. This leaves open the possibility that people of faith identify as Christians, Hindus, Muslims, and as followers of other religions (a term he did not find useful) and challenges those who claim superiority for their system. Might I discern real faith in Muslim lives and hearts? Despite his deep recognition of Muslim piety at the personal level, Cragg attracted criticism for addressing an allegedly abstract Islam that will one day metamorphize into Christianity toward which it has always pointed. Finally, another tutor, whose classes I attended during 1978–79, was fellow Baptist Barbara M. Boal, who taught tribal religions and cultures. After serving with BMS in India

---

4. Cragg, *Pen and the Faith*, 109.

among tribal peoples, Boal obtained her doctorate in anthropology from Edinburgh University. BMS wanted me to attend her course because, while Bangladesh has a Muslim majority, many Christians belong to various aboriginal peoples. Boal's classes gave me some awareness of basic ethnography as a process of observing, listening, and learning in order to understand a people and their culture from the inside, which in many respects became the task I set myself in Bangladesh. In fact, the process started in Selly Oak when I carried out some field work among the expatriate Bangladeshi community for my dissertation on Islam in Bangladesh, especially focusing on the role that Ṣūfīs played in Islam's spread there. Since then I have worked extensively on the nature of Ṣūfism in Bangladesh, and on the role it has played as a bridge between religions and communities. My contributions to two volumes on Ṣūfism, which I coedited, contain the result of this work. The concept of rigid boundaries between religious communities may itself be a Western construct.

Bangladesh: My Journey Continues

After several months on leave with my parents in Australia, I reached Bangladesh in October 1979. My first year was spent in full-time language study at the Oriental Institute in Barisal. I traveled down river from Dhaka on an old steamer affectionately known, ironically, given its sedate speed, as the *Rocket*. To my surprise, a leftover from colonial days still allowed me to travel as a missionary in first class with a large discount. This was a reminder that missionaries in the days of the British Raj were sometimes regarded as an embarrassment by other, better-paid British personnel who did not want fellow expatriates to be seen traveling second or third class. The trip downriver was an eye-opener, too, because while Selly Oak had prepared me for encountering extreme poverty and experiencing what was called "culture shock," no one had thought to tell me that Bangladesh is also a very beautiful, green, vibrant country. The language program was intensive. For the first six months or so I lodged at the institute. This was run by the Catholic Congregation of the Holy Cross. The well-kept grounds, with a water tank where we swam, was a very pleasant environment for study and reflection. Later, the family living in the mission house at Chanmari, the main Baptist compound in the city, which included a boys and a girls boarding school, left and I took their place. We studied Bengali literature, as well as learning vocabulary and conversational language. I did not know this at the time but my future wife, Rekha Sarker, was a student at the girls school. I may have seen her, because the boys and girls would march, in their uniforms, into the church for Sunday worship. There were about forty BMS personnel working in Bangladesh at this time engaged in a variety of tasks including health care, supervising the construction of buildings, running an agricultural project, and serving the churches of the Baptist Church Sangha as pastors and theological teachers. I was to serve in the latter capacity. At the end of a year, I passed the Junior Language Examination (conducted by a board formed by various mission bodies), which meant that I could assume official duties while continuing with Bengali study part time in preparation for taking the Senior Examination. I was transferred to Khulna, sailing overnight on the *Rocket* and occupying a bungalow on the main mission compound. Most of this was leased to a Japanese agricultural not-for-profit. I was pastor of the central church at Koilaghat, but a recent split within the membership meant that a rival group controlled the building. We worshipped in another space. The Senior Examination included submitting a special project. Mine was an annotated translation of John's gospel in the Muslim-nuanced form of Bengali. Christians, whose background is mostly Hindu, use a more Sanskritic form. I now led worship regularly and preached both at the central church and out in surrounding villages. I conducted several baptisms, too. At the end of that year I successfully passed the Senior Language examination.

Lewis Bevan Jones had written about problems associated with Muslim converts in terms of how well the Christian community receives and treats them in an appendix to the 1939 Calcutta edition of *The People of the Mosque* (original, 1932). "The Christian Church . . . as a whole and as a rule," he wrote, "does not cordially welcome the convert from Islam."[5] I experienced this firsthand when a young man presented himself as a new Christian at the door of the mission house. His conversion left him without a job or a home because his employer and family had disowned him. He became my *peon* (messenger). The local Christians were unhappy, saying that Muslims like him could not be trusted. They pretended to be converts, took jobs from Christians, married their women, then reverted, taking their wives with them into the Muslim community. Sadly, after several months, the young man stole my bicycle and absconded. Whatever I thought about the imperative or otherwise of bringing Muslims into membership of church, this experience told me that lessons still needed to be learned

---

5. Jones, *People of the Mosque* (1939 ed.), 317.

despite almost two hundred years of the BMS working in East Bengal. On the one hand, local Christians spoke much about the duty of witnessing to Muslims. They were suspicious of someone such as myself whom they saw as potentially compromising with Islam. On the other hand, this experience suggested that what Jones described decades ago still happened. In year three, I was stationed at Rangpur, in the Northwest. The compound was also home to a Lutheran World Service appropriate technology project. I represented the Rangpur Baptist *Sammilani* (Association) on the national Mission and Ministry committee, supervised the Christian bookstore, and taught for the Theological Education by Extension program of the College of Christian Theology, which BMS supported. This included tutoring diploma students but also running basic Christian education programs for village churches where most of our members were from two *Adibashi* (Aboriginal) communities. It was in Rangpur that I developed better relations with Muslims especially by visiting the Islamic Studies department at the local government college, where I expressed interest in registering for an MA. While in Bangladesh, I completed several credits by distance learning in the MA in missiology through the Fuller Theological Seminary, Pasadena, California, but found the idea of gaining a masters in Islamic studies at a Bangladesh institution appealing. Unfortunately, this did not attract the necessary support and I began thinking about returning to Birmingham to pursue an MA there. Fuller required a residential component, which made completing their degree financially unviable. However, I learned a lot about the history and methods of Christian mission from the courses. Much use was made of Kenneth Scott Latourette's *A History of the Expansion of Christianity*. I was also introduced to the church-growth thought of Donald McGravan (1897–1990), dean and professor of mission at Fuller.

My Observation of Muslim Life in Bangladesh

On the one hand, it sometimes appeared that Christians in Bangladesh kept apart from Muslims. They tended to live in their own neighborhoods, many worked for Christian organizations or ran business that mainly relied on Christian patronage. The churches remained largely dependent on overseas financial aid to maintain their large compounds and run the educational and health care institutions that had been handed over when, theoretically, local leadership succeeded that of missionaries in post-independence East Pakistan. I encountered criticism from some colleagues when I began paying my domestic servants higher salaries than Bangladeshi pastors received because I did not feel comfortable paying them the customary rate. I thought then and think now that the pattern of full-time, salaried ministry and of expensive buildings inherited from Europe might not be the most appropriate model of being church for a developing country. In fact, here in the United States, many congregations are challenged by the financial costs of paying their pastors and keeping church doors open, maintaining ways of being church that may no longer make sense. This dependence led some Muslims to see Christians as agents of the West. I was in Bangladesh during the Iran hostage crisis and once, walking in a village with a Christian friend, heard him being repeatedly asked where he "came from." He kept saying "Barisal," to which his questioner replied, "No, you are a Christian, so where do you come from," implying that he could not possibly be a Christian and a native of Bangladesh. Compared to how Ṣūfīs had transplanted Islam into the cultural soil of Bengal, Christianity could have been dropped ready made in European form from a helicopter! Bengal was the first mission field for English Baptists, beginning in 1793 with William Carey himself (founder of the BMS), which means that Baptists have had time to acculturate Christianity more than they have. On the other hand, I knew Christians who had very good relations with Muslims and my own conversations with them informed me how much they valued the schools and hospitals that Christians run, considered among the best. The Baptist Sangha's president, Michael Sushil Adhikari (1924–1997), was a state minister and later a senior advisor to the government. Almost all Muslims with whom I spoke did not understand the distinctions between Christian denominations; they would immediately begin talking about a missionary they knew who inevitably turned out to be Catholic. My attempts to explain that my mission was Baptist not Catholic produced expressions of bafflement suggesting that there was little point pursuing this. Very often, my conversations included some discussion of basic differences between Islam and Christianity usually centered on Jesus as God's son and on the Trinity. Muslims would tell me that God is One, and Jesus is a prophet. Yet when we parted, they often stated, "Well, you and I worship the same God," more or less citing Qur'ān 29:46 and expressed friendly best wishes. This contrasts with the claim encountered in some Christian writing that the God of Islam, and the God of the Bible, are different, one a revengeful, angry God, the other a loving one. Mosques and Ṣūfī shrines continue to thrive in Bangladesh. I saw—then and on more recent visits—little evidence that

Islamist or radical Islam had widespread support, although it certainly exists there. During my field work in Birmingham I had learned about the popular *Tablīghī Jamā'at*, a neo-Ṣūfī organization that retains elements of Ṣūfī practice but rejects saint and shrine veneration. *Tablīghī* members do not discuss politics. This seems to me to represent a typical viewpoint in Bangladesh. My impression is that most Bangladeshis value Islam as their devotional and spiritual practice but do not think that government must be distinctly Islamic. In fact, Bangladesh was founded as a secular state (1972). This principle, removed from the constitution in 1977, was restored in 2011. Islamist parties have failed to win more than a handful of seats in successive elections. Bangladeshis whether Muslim, Hindu, Buddhist, or Christian are proud of their common cultural legacy of poetry, music, plays, and more recently, cinematography. My sister-in-law, Roji Sarker, is a much admired singer of Bāul songs. Traditionally sung by mendicant minstrels with Hindu and Muslim backgrounds, this music continues to bring people together across different religious identities.

Return to Birmingham

By late 1982, I had returned to Birmingham. I spent October 1982 to January 1983 working on a cooperative farm in Israel and touring sacred and historical sites. During that period I also visited the occupied territories for the first time spending Christmas Eve and Christmas morning in Bethlehem. In 1983, I registered for the MA by research through CSIC under David Kerr and began writing my dissertation on Lewis Bevan Jones. When I went to Bangladesh I thought that would be a long-term assignment. Before long, however, I realized that I needed to pursue academic goals in order to work through theological issues that I felt I had to address. Those of us who are called to serve need to be open to God calling us away from one venture into another! I think of the voice from Macedonia that deflected Paul from his plan of journeying into Asia (Acts 16:9). As I describe my various jobs in this chapter I skip over the fact that there has been no real plan! I have accepted opportunities as they presented themselves—whether prestigious or obscure—if they enabled me to engage in what I prayerfully consider useful to God's purposes. However, on July 2, 2018, when I preached on my fortieth ordination anniversary, I did point to a pattern—my jobs have all involved building bridges and challenging misconceptions between people of different races and religions.

INTRODUCTION—MY PERSONAL JOURNEY

In 1983, I was able to secure some bursaries but needed to find employment to cover cost of accommodation. The Baptist Union granted me two years leave of absence from active ministry. Early in 1983, I attended an event on jobs and employment at Birmingham Cathedral where I first met the then general secretary of Birmingham Council of Christian Churches (BCCC), Ultan Russell, who became a close friend. He told me about a new not-for-profit, the Birmingham Ethnic Education and Advisory Service (BEEAS), set up by P. C. Chakravarti, MBE former principal community relations officer for Birmingham, which was working mainly with the Bangladeshi diaspora encouraging neighborhood self-help and educational programs. From West Bengal, Chakravarti, known as David, was interested in recruiting a Bengali speaker and had floated the possibility that a non-Bengali might be well placed to avoid political entanglements within the community. This sounded like a job designed with me in mind. It was a part-time position, which was ideal for my purposes. The task was to contact people in the community—door-to-door visits were involved—invite them to meetings to discuss forming self-help neighborhood associations and the type of activities they would like organized. These always included learning English for women and Bengali classes for children. We then found venues where classes could be held and secured funding for these. A lot of my work took me into local schools where activities were often located. Daily speaking Bengali ensured my continued love of the language, culture, and people of Bangladesh. With minimal preparation, I sat for the Bengali "o" Level in 1985, gaining an A grade. It often seemed as though I was still living in Bangladesh. I saw a lot of continuity between my work in Bangladesh and among the diaspora community. There are Bangladeshi families in my part of New York State, too, where a nearby school district has enough Bangladeshi students to invite me to run a language immersion program for their teachers. I know a number of these families. Recently, at a meeting of the National Muslim-Christian Initiative in the United States a Bangladeshi member described me as a "son-in-law of Bangladesh."

Before long I was co-opted onto a governing body of one of the schools that hosted activities. I spent a great deal of time visiting mosques, especially Birmingham Central Mosque, where one of my coworkers was a trustee. I became skilled at writing constitutions that passed the Charity Commission's scrutiny for registration, and found myself drafting several for mosques and other local organizations. I also helped mosques obtain permission to conduct marriages. I secured funding for and helped

INTRODUCTION—MY PERSONAL JOURNEY

organize vacation children's schemes, including seaside trips for children and families. Most funds were from two government initiatives, the Inner City Partnership and the Manpower Services Commission's Community program. I became a member of Highgate Baptist Church, very close to Birmingham Central Mosque, and was elected a deacon there. When I graduated MA July 11, 1985, (internal examiner, Sigvard von Sicard; external, Jan Slomp), my leave from ministry expired and the Baptist Union recognized me as associate pastor of the Highgate church, a position I held until September 1992. The BU also paid half of my PhD tuition fees. At Highgate, I organized exchange visits between the mosque and ourselves, which I wrote up for the *Baptist Times*.[6] In 1986, when the mosque applied for permission to broadcast the call to prayer from its minaret (which the original planning permission did not allow) the local parish church, which opposed this on the grounds that only Anglicans could issue a summons for prayer (by ringing bells), invited me to advocate for the mosque. I also became chair of governors at the local primary school. Heavily involved in the Birmingham Council of Christian Churches (BCCC), I sat on the executive committee, chaired the Birmingham Affairs Committee (which liaised with the city and the West Midlands Police Service), and represented the BCCC on the Community Relations and Interfaith Councils and on the Court of Birmingham University. Lesslie Newbigin was one of three BCCC vice presidents at this time. When he retired, I gave the vote of thanks. Within my own denomination, I served on the Baptist District committee and on the West Midlands Baptist Association General Committee. I was also an advisor to the National Council for Lay Associations of the Catholic Bishops Conference taking part in two European Forum meetings in Austria and Belgium, which further extended my ecumenical involvement. On behalf of the Interfaith Council I organized visits to temples, churches, and mosques during One World Weeks. One was recorded for a BBC radio program. Shortly after graduating MA, I registered for my PhD. I also became part-time Free Church chaplain at Aston University, leaving BEEAS, although continuing to engage in the same type of community development as chair of the Bengali Association in my own neighborhood. Highlights include attending the 1987 *Kirchentag* as one of a hundred guests from the BCCC in Frankfurt and cohosting visits by Desmond Tutu during Birmingham's centennial celebrations and by Cardinal Arinze, then president of the Pontifical Council for Interreligious Dialogue, on an official visit to the UK.

6. Bennett, "Day the Baptists Met the Muslims."

I rode with him to the Catholic Seminary at Oscott, Birmingham, under police escort, which, because we were running late, caused the lights to change so that we could speed along the central emergency lane! I also met the former world champion boxer and civil rights activist Muhammad Ali when he spoke at an event organized by the Community Relations Council.

Some of my activities attracted criticism. My helping mosques obtain charitable status, planning permissions and funding was seen as a betrayal of Christian faith! One critic said that until Saudi Arabia permits Christians to build churches we should not assist Muslims with their mosques in the UK. He called for reciprocity. I was once described at a meeting (I was not present but heard of this later) as someone who bent over "black-wards" and passed over for a post as advisor to the inner-city Baptist congregations. However, I developed lasting, deep friendships with many Muslims during this period. I remember typing away late one evening on an old manual machine drafting a constitution in the upper room of a house mosque surrounded by Muslim friends, being acutely conscious of how unique this experience probably was. One Muslim friend, who I helped edit several books on the history of Bangladeshi migration to the UK, introduced me to my future wife, Rekha.

At the British Council of Churches

The Aston post was a one-year contract while the future of Free Church chaplaincy at Birmingham's higher education institutions was under review. While there, I began an initiative that led to the denominations involved in the chaplaincy entering a formal ecumenical covenant. During 1987, a position at the British Council of Churches' Community and Race Relations Unit (CRRU), for which Ultan Russel had previously worked, became vacant and I applied. I was interviewed but not chosen. However, the BCC informed me that another position, more suitable, would soon become vacant. That turned out to be the post of executive officer of the Committee for Relations with People of Other Faiths in the Mission Division of the Council. CROPOF (as the committee was known) was funded by mission agencies. Kenneth Cracknell, whose term had ended, was the first to hold this position. This time my application succeeded and I took up my duties at headquarters in London in August 1987, although I kept my home in Birmingham, continuing at Highgate, on BCCC and other committees. A CROPOF member, who was superintendent of Whitechapel

Methodist Mission, rented me accommodation at a subsidized rate at the mission, which meant that I could sleep there whenever needed. This became my second home. Whitehall is one of the most multireligious and multicultural areas in Britain. The famous Brick Lane Mosque was a short walk away. Originally a church for French Protestant refugees (1734), it later became a synagogue and finally, as demographics changed, a mosque. This serves the predominantly Bangladeshi community of what is often called Bangla Town. Street signs in the Brick Lane area are in Bangla and English. Salman Rushdie's *The Satanic Verses*' setting of "Brickhall" conflated London's Southall, Brixton, and Brick Lane. The novel refers to the mosque as a former Calvinist church and synagogue.[7] Monica Ali's novel *Brick Lane* (2003), and the film (2007, directed by Sarah Gavron), are also set there. My committee chair (moderator), the Right Reverend Jim Thompson (1936–2003), then bishop of Stepney, conveniently lived a short distance from the mission.

My post at the BCC involved attending the committees of those member churches that had established interfaith advisory bodies including the Methodist Church, the United Reformed Church, the Roman Catholic Bishops Conference of England and Wales, and the Church of England. I also served on the executive committees of the Council of Christians and Jews, the World Congress of Faiths, and the newly established Interfaith Network. During the CCJ's jubilee anniversary celebration I was presented, with other members of the executive, to the organization's patron, Her Majesty Queen Elizabeth II, at a reception in St. James Palace. Through the Interfaith Network (founded 1987) I developed very good relations with Dr. Zaki Badawi, KBE (1922–2006), former imam of the Regents Park Mosque and founder of the Muslim College, London. Zaki and I issued several joint press statements during my time at BCC, including responses to the Rushdie affair and the Gulf War of 1990–1991. Zaki defended Rushdie's freedom of speech, arguing that Muslims who found the book offensive should write a critique, or ignore it, not try to kill him. I wrote several essays on the Rushdie affair editing a volume of CROPOF's journal, *Discernment*,[8] on the topic. We both thought that diplomacy had not been exhausted before use of military force began in Iraq. Many British Muslims found themselves at odds with public opinion in the UK on these issues, which generated some hostility toward them. It was at meetings in Selly Oak convened annually

---

7. Rushdie, *Satanic Verses*, 294.
8. "Focus on the Salman Rushdie Affair," *Discernment*, 4:2.

by the CROPF vice moderator, Canon Christopher Lamb, that I first met Farid Esack, whose work I admire. At the time, he was researching his doctorate at CSIC. Lamb invited him to attend a meeting of what we called British Missionary Islamicists. We were all Islamic studies specialists who also operated as Christian theologians with interests in missiology. Other members included Martin Forward, then director of Interfaith Relations for the Methodist Church, David Thomas of CSIC, Hugh Goddard, now at Edinburgh University, Neal Robinson, whose publications include *Christ in Islam and Christianity* (1991), and Nancy Lambton (1912–2008), professor for many years at SOAS and a former press attaché at the British Embassy in Iran. Esack was one of two Muslims whom we invited to join our discussions; the other, Ataullah Siddiqui, author of *Muslims in Dialogue with Christians* (1996) now professor of Christian-Muslim Relations and Interfaith Understanding at Markfield Institute of Higher Education (a fully accredited Islamic college, founded 2000) kindly wrote this book's foreword. CROPOF's four subgroups all edited an issue of the journal *Discernment* during my tenure. At my commissioning service, I predicted that the work of the Social Policy subgroup would become vital as debate on what it means to be British in a culturally and religiously plural society developed. That subgroup's chair, Archy Kirkwoord, then an MP, now Baron Kirkwood of Kirhhope, sometimes arranged for us to meet at the Houses of Parliament.

As a Practitioner of Dialogue

I attended various meetings of the World Council of Churches Sub-Unit on Dialogue with Living Faiths and Ideologies, including two, both in Switzerland, as part of the drafting team for *Issues in Christian-Muslim Relations: Ecumenical Consideration* (1991). This experience helped develop my understanding of the dynamics and aims of interfaith dialogue. The subunit published a paper I wrote, "Dialogue, Witness or Treason" (1988). I regard myself as a practitioner of dialogue as described in the WCC's *Guidelines* (1979) but especially as redacted by Cracknell and CROPOF into four principles first published, with commentary, in 1981. These are:

1. Dialogue begins when people meet each other;
2. Dialogue depends on mutual trust and mutual understanding;
3. Dialogue makes it possible to share in service to the community;

INTRODUCTION—MY PERSONAL JOURNEY

4. Dialogue becomes the medium of authentic witness.

Much of my work at CROPOF involved encouraging member churches to adopt these at synods, conventions, assemblies, or conferences and producing a new explanatory publication, *In Good Faith* (1991). While at CROPOF, I read widely in theology of religions. I knew of John Hick's *God and the Universe of Faiths* (1973)[9] and of his pluralist proposition from my initial days at Selly Oak. However, it was CROPOF member Alan Race who had popularized use of the paradigms, exclusivism, inclusivism, and pluralism, to describe three theologies of religion in his *Christians and Religious Pluralism: Patterns in the Christian Theology of Religions* (1983). The first limits salvation to those who explicitly declare faith in Jesus and represents the thinking of the church in which I was nurtured; the second regards Jesus' role in salvation as central but does not restrict this to self-defined Christians, drawing on the possibility that implicit faith may also be saving; while the third sees all faiths as valid alternative paths to spiritual fulfilment. The exclusivist paradigm had dominated mission thinking since the Tambaram World Mission Conference of 1938. Mahatma Gandhi, said Hendrik Kraemer (1888–1965), who proposed the exclusivist paradigm at the conference, might be a good man but he was a Hindu and therefore unsaved.[10] Persuading people to become Christian, to abandon existing faiths if they have one, is not only the goal of mission but a task of great urgency lest the End come and billions of souls perish. Numbers matter. Good works must take a secondary place, as should fully forming new converts, because both divert resources from the primary mission. Nothing must hinder adding numbers to the church. The church-growth movement, pioneered by McGravan, developed from this logic. The second paradigm more or less became official Roman Catholic thinking after Vatican II due to the influence of Karl Rahner (1904–1984). This leaves salvation to God, which is available to all people because of Jesus' life, death, and resurrection but does not require explicit faith in Christ. The third, associated with John Hick (1922–2012), with whom I later served on the board of the Oxford International Interfaith Centre during my time at Westminster College, Oxford, could perhaps be described as a post-Christian or post-Christian imperialism option, similar in some respects to death of God theology. I last heard Hick speak in 2003, when he gave a public lecture during the Pluralism

---

9. Citations are from the 1993 reissue.
10. Hogg, "Christian Attitude," 109–13.

Summit, held September 6–9 at Birmingham University. He predicted that pluralism would end up attracting the support of most Christians, drawing an analogy between how Christians had opposed the concept of biological evolution, which in the end has generally prevailed even among Christians. Similarly, religious pluralism will prevail because it is necessary in our postmodern world for peace and coexistence. Pluralists, says Hick, see "the great world faiths, including Christianity" as "different and independently authentic spheres of revelation and salvation."[11] The largest Baptist denomination, though, the Southern Baptist Convention, regards evolution as scientifically unproven and calls for the teaching of creation science in public schools.[12]

At this time, a flurry of publications on interfaith relations led one colleague to express jealousy that money seemed to be available for this "growth industry" rather than for their field of lay education, although CROPOF was not especially well funded and neither were most interfaith bodies at the time. CCJ was facing a financial crisis which alarmed those of us who served on its executive where the question of liability was raised. However, Tambaram's fiftieth anniversary stimulated more interest and theological contributions. In missionary circles, much discussion centered on whether the dialogical approach compromised or even betrayed mission, which had stimulated my WCC paper. Newbigin's *Gospel in a Pluralist Society* appeared in 1989. This was very much a response to the contemporary conversation on Christianity in relation to the world's religions. What attracted me was how my former teacher offered an alternative rationale for mission to one of "stemming the fearful cataract of souls going into eternal perdition"[13] by criticizing the three-paradigm approach yet at the same time embracing an aspect of each position. Also, he rooted this in biblical exegesis. As a Baptist, it remains normative for me to try to establish biblical grounds for theological ideas. He wrote:

> [My] position is *exclusivist* in the sense that it affirms the unique truth of the revelation in Jesus Christ, but it is not exclusivist in the sense of denying the possibility of the salvation of the non-Christian. It is *inclusivist* in the sense that it refuses to limit the saving grace of God to the members of the Christian church, but it

---

11. Hick, *Universe of Faith*, vii.

12. Resolution on Scientific Creationism (1982), available at http://www.sbc.net/resolutions/967.

13. Newbigin, *Gospel in a Pluralist Society*, 124–25.

rejects the inclusivism which regards the non-Christian religions as vehicles of salvation. It is *pluralist* in the sense of acknowledging the gracious work of God in the lives of all human beings, but it rejects a pluralism which denies the uniqueness and decisiveness of what God has done in Jesus Christ.[14]

Examining the New Testament, Newbigin simply did not find there the same concern for results or anxiety about numbers that characterizes church-growth thought. Paul, he pointed out, never agonizes about results. Instead, in one of his most profoundly missiological passages, he speaks of salvation in eschatological terms and suggests that no one is perfect until the end. God "has consigned all people to disobedience in order that he may have mercy on all" (Rom 11:32–36). It is at the End, says Newbigin, that "the fathomless depths of God's wisdom and grace will be revealed."[15] Meanwhile, "creation groans in travail" (Rom 8:22). Thus, Christians should be neither anxious about their failure or boast about their success, but should faithfully witness "to the one in whom the whole purpose of God for cosmic history has been revealed."[16] Newbigin preferred to speak of the "logic of mission," predicated on the truthfulness of the message as one that cannot but be proclaimed (or, as I prefer "shared"). We do not control the result. This is the Holy Spirit's task. Some people may join the church, others may respond in ways that are invisible to us. Newbigin does not say that mere proclamation is enough; proclamation must be persuasive and culturally sensitive. Evangelists should use strategies which have proven effective while resisting the temptation to control the process. Converts, too, Newbigin argued, must be aware of the ethical dimension of the gospel, thus "discipling" and "perfecting" cannot be so easily separated. Lacking knowledge of the ethical dimension, converts will focus only on replicating their conversion in others. They will ignore the gospel command to heal the sick, liberate the oppressed, give sight to the blind, to restore the world to its original perfection (Luke 4:18–20), for only such a world will be acceptable to God. This challenged insistence by church-growth practitioners that social programs and time spent on "perfecting" diverts effort and resources from the more urgent evangelical task. Highgate, where I was still serving as associate pastor, was funded from the Baptist Union's Home Mission program. Each year, we had to justify continued support and the

---

14. Newbigin, *Gospel in a Pluralist Society*, 182–83.
15. Newbigin, *Gospel in a Pluralist Society*, 125.
16. Newbigin, *Gospel in a Pluralist Society*, 125.

main criterion used for this was how many new members had joined. The local population was disproportionately elderly, which meant that our statistics were unimpressive. Even though we did attract newcomers they often replaced members who had passed away. The fact that we provided a wide range of social services to the local community did nothing to help us meet the criterion for funding yet arguably we were undertaking biblically mandated mission as faithfully as wealthy churches in suburbia were, which did grow numerically. The value of our socially engaged mission went unmeasured.

Newbigin allowed the possibility that Muslims as Muslims and Hindus as Hindus may be saved. This does sound like Rahner's "if one believes in the universal salvific purposes of God toward all men in Christ, it need not and really cannot be doubted that gratuitous influences of properly Christian supernatural grace are conceivable in the life of all men."[17] Thus, a non-Christian may experience "the grace of God" without knowing that this grace is being mediated through Jesus Christ. Dialogue begins when people meet each other. Christians who denigrate other faiths often do so from a distance. In contrast, dialogue takes place face-to-face. Yet as conceived by the ecumenical movement that has more or less endorsed interfaith dialogue, it does not preclude but enables Christian witness. What, then, should we make of a verse such as John 14:6, one of several Bible verses often cited as a proof text against inclusivism? In my opinion, this refers to Jesus as the one through whom all that God saves are imputed righteousness not to the necessity of naming him before the Day of Reckoning, when all the redeemed in Christ will finally name him as Lord (Phil 2:10). All those who walk the way of truth, justice, and peace are Jesus' disciples whether they name him now or on that day. Salvation "in no other name" (Acts 4:6) need not be repudiated.

Proposing a Revised Soteriology Consistent with the Baptist Evangelical Legacy

The fourth CROPOF principle states that dialogue becomes a medium of authentic witness. This means that we can share our deepest faith convictions and spiritual experiences with our partners, whose response might be to embrace Christianity just as ours might be to embrace their religious faith. My view is that dialogue does not preclude proclamation but enables

17. Rahner, "Non-Christian Religions," 125.

faith sharing in ways that are more likely to attract a positive response from hearers than expressions of hostility toward what they already believe. I regard salvation as God's work through the Holy Spirit. In practice, though, it becomes a human work too because it depends both on a preacher proclaiming the gospel and on hearers responding, making a decision for Christ. The Holy Spirit may be understood as inspiring the proclamation and the response but if there is no human choice involved at all our souls lack freedom. It would seem problematic, too, to reconcile belief in what my Baptist forbears call "soul competency" with the idea of some that only an elect is saved since those elected have no say in the matter. Hick saw this as a denial of divine love, asking, "Can we accept the conclusion that the God of love who seeks to save all mankind has nevertheless ordained that men must be saved in such a way that only a small minority can in fact receive this salvation?"[18] Equally, to believe that God predestined people's damnation also undermines human freedom. Perhaps a combination of Calvinists' insistence on salvation as God's free gift with the need for a human turning toward God would preserve "soul competency" and the inviolability of the unfettered conscience. Famously, Charles Haddon Spurgeon (1834–1892) said on several occasions when fellow Calvinists criticized his frequent altar calls inviting sinners to repent that God should call all his elect and then elect some more.[19] If we separate faith, as God's free gift of grace from both the work of sharing the gospel and from the individual's free response to this, the possibility that anyone who turns to God will find themselves embraced by God's limitless love remains open. They may turn to God as a practicing Hindu or Muslim and experience spiritual renewal without becoming Christian. Failure to share may mean that some miss the opportunity to discover the faith tradition that will best nourish them, so while we should not agonize about results there is a duty involved here. I readily admit here that while for me faith is God's unearned gift, a faith that does not express itself through works is dead (Jas 2:17), a view that Calvin in fact espoused. For him, good works do not earn salvation but they do signify likely membership of the elect. Calvin wrote:

> We forbid no believer to confirm and support this faith by the signs of the divine favor towards him. For if when we call to mind the gifts which God has bestowed upon us, they are like rays of the divine countenance, by which we are enabled to behold the

18. Hick, *Universe of Faith*, 122–23.
19. Fisk, *Election and Predestination*, 69.

highest light of his goodness; much more is this the case with the gift of good works, which shows that we have received the Spirit of adoption.[20]

I remember Michael Taylor, though, saying that he had no interest in a salvation to which he could make no contribution and have more than a little sympathy with this view. Inclusivists say that salvation is always mediated by Jesus whether he is acknowledged or not, which pluralists say sounds like theological imperialism. On the other hand, my friend Farid Esack's work offers a similar proposition from an Islamic perspective.[21] Peoples' inner faith and outer acts may qualify them as "muslim" although they remain outside the Muslim community. Cragg's soul-searching struggle to make theological sense of Islam *as a Christian*, for me, represents the golden standard in my chosen field. Arguably, while engaging in religious dialogue, it would be a failure of sharing for a Christian to remain silent about that which they treasure above everything, their spiritual experience, that which gives life meaning, purpose, and value. Leaving salvation to the Holy Spirit means that some will respond in ways we recognize as Christian while others do so "in ways which no third party will ever understand."[22]

This works best when we ground what we share in our personal experience, rather than insist on exact doctrinal formulations. For example, on Trinity, I will argue in this book (drawing on Jones), we can speak about how our experience of the divine finds expression through Trinitarian language, rather than dogmatize on the absolute need to subscribe to the Nicene Creed. This is certainly consistent with my own Baptist non-creedal tradition. God may be Three in One, One without any Persons, or perhaps manifested in three hundred and thirty million ways as Hindus say, but ultimately God is irreducible to any number. Jones pointed out, too, "that no Christian claims that even the most widely accepted definition of the Trinity is adequate to the ultimate truth about God, but we do claim that it is a contribution to a better understanding of the mystery of His Nature."[23] Perhaps we need to think of our theological ideas as wholly true about God and the divine-human relationship yet not the whole truth, leaving room to learn from others' theologies. Unless we think that we are God's equal, there should be room for mystery, even paradox and ambiguity yet this we

20. Calvin, *Institutes*, 343.
21. See Esack, *Qur'an, Liberation & Pluralism*.
22. Newbigin, *Gospel in a Pluralist Society*, 182.
23. Jones, *Christianity Explained*, 94–95.

know, God's spirit moves within us. Some of our differences may confound and perplex us. Yet collaborating with Hindus and Muslims on making the world peaceful, just, equitable, and sustainable might end up pleasing God more than theological disputation which the Qur'ān strongly implies (5:48). When Jesus began his ministry, he said that he had come to release prisoners, give sight to the blind, and to announce the coming of God's kingdom. Kingdom building, what I call the Lukan mandate, may be our missiological calling, the *missio Dei*. Yet, as we labor alongside people of other faiths and those of none, we still have a mandate and a responsibility to share our experience of spiritual renewal even as we listen to those of others. While I uphold anyone's right to disbelieve in God as fervently as I do people's right to believe, I suspect that some atheists and agnostics who place others' genuine needs above their own, live simply that others might simply live by eating enough for their need not greed (a Gandhi aphorism) may on the other side of death yet have a chance to accept God's love. On Hick, whose writing and speeches I always found engaging, I disagree with his rejection of revelation although some have described me as his disciple. I believe in a God who discloses, reveals, and communicates God's will and purposes to humanity but also that this is subject to human interpretation and misunderstanding.

After the BCC

During my first three years at BCC, the inter-church process was discussing how to move ecumenism forward in terms of a structure that some churches not yet affiliated—principally the Roman Catholic Bishops Conferences in England and Wales, in Scotland and in Ireland—might join. This led to the formation of a new body, in succession to the BCC, initially called the Council of Churches for Britain and Ireland (CCBI, now Churches Together in Britain and Ireland). I worked for the CCBI for the last two years of my term, which ended in 1992. I completed my PhD in December 1989, graduating July 12, 1990. David Kerr had moved to Hartford Seminary, Connecticut, USA, by then (where Cragg had taught earlier). I flew out to Connecticut to consult him before submitting my dissertation, published as *Victorian Images of Islam* (1992). Christian Troll, SJ, became my official supervisor for the last two years of research. Again, von Sicard was my internal examiner. My external was C. E. Bosworth (1928–2015). Frances Young chaired the defense. In my dissertation, I explored how theological presuppositions color and shape Christian writing on Islam all but determining how they see Islam whether in a way that stresses affinity or difference. I categorized approaches as confrontational or conciliatory. Edward Said's *Orientalism* (1978) was a major influence, as was W. C. Smith's dictum that the task of a Christian writing on Islam is to attract Muslims' approval.[24]

In 1992, I left CCBI to join Westminster College, Oxford, as a lecturer in the study of religions (later senior lecturer), resident tutor, and assistant chaplain, remaining there until 1998. I was appointed to focus on Islam in my teaching and also to develop an anthropological approach—which led me to develop further my interest in ethnography in part by completing a master of education which used social science and qualitative research (awarded by Oxford University, October 5, 1996). This continued work I had undertaken for the Oxford Professional Qualification in teaching and learning in higher education, which I was awarded after my first academic year at Westminster to meet a government requirement. I cowrote *Researching into Teaching Methods* (1996) drawing on my MEd dissertation. I added the Fellowship of the Royal Anthropological Institute to my existing Fellowship of the Royal Asiatic Society at this time to boost my credentials. This interest also informed my 1996 text, *In Search of the Sacred: Anthropology and the Study of Religion*. I spent a succession of summers living at the Henry Martyn Institute in Hyderabad and teaching a summer school in Bangalore for an MTh program Westminster offered in India in partnership with TAFTEE (The Association for Theological Education by Extension). I also carried out fieldwork research in Bangladesh during visits to my wife's family there. At Westminster, I continued to edit the journal *Discernment* and represented the Baptist Union on the World Council of Churches' Consultation on the Church and the Jewish People attending meetings in Geneva and Budapest. After Westminster, I was an associate professor of religion, specializing in Islam at Baylor University, Texas, between 1998 and 2001. Next, a hiatus in my career saw me working at a community school in Birmingham where over 95 percent of students were Muslim while researching my book *Muslims and Modernity* (2005) as an honorary Fellow at Birmingham University and teaching on a very part-time basis for the Centre for the Study of Judaism and Jewish-Christian Relations, Cambridge. At the school, I regularly led Islamic collective worship at the invitation of Muslim colleagues. My interfaith activism continued, too. In

24. Smith, "Comparative Religion," 43.

2005, I returned to the United States, where I have now taught religious and Asian studies for over a decade at the State University of New York at New Paltz. Situated in a historic village in the scenic Mid-Hudson Valley settled by Huguenot refugees in 1678, the college's origin lies in a classics school founded in 1828. Over the years, while my specialty remains South Asian Islam, I have also maintained close interest in the Middle East. At New Paltz, I became involved in the Center for Middle Eastern Dialogue, which organizes seminars and conferences, when it began in 2008 under the then dean of the College of Liberal Arts and Sciences, Professor James Schiffer. I also served as president of the Lifetime Learning Institute 2014–2015.

I acquired US citizenship in 2012. Also in 2012, I became a Recognized Clergyperson of the Alliance of Baptists, a small Baptist denomination whose stated principles and commitments very much align with my own. Although in good standing with the Baptist Union of Great Britain in 2011, I no longer qualified for retention on the list of accredited clergy so affiliated with the Alliance. We call the Alliance "a theological home in pursuit of God's justice, and partnership in mission." For me, the Alliance provides a Baptist association of which I am very proud because of its commitment to social justice, equity, collegiality, and diversity. Locally, however, I joined the fittingly named Clinton Avenue United Methodist Church in Kingston, New York, where I later became interim pastor and am now a trustee and member of the pastoral team. I preach there most Sundays. Until recently, our church ran a daily food program, a food bank, and hosted a range of community services including a legal advice clinic and High School Equivalency classes (formerly known as GED, the General Education Diploma). We are now in a transitional period as we work with a local not-for-profit to renovate the building for more extensive community use and so have had to close the kitchen (which the Salvation Army has taken over). We are active within Kingston Interfaith Council, too, which has become the venue where clergy meet rather than through the moribund local Council of Churches. The Interfaith Council is currently coordinating volunteers to help run the County Warming Center, which we hosted until entering the transitional period. We also rent some of our premises to a Buddhist inspired community outreach substance abuse recovery agency.

The alliance ratified a statement on Muslim-Christian relations, the first by a Baptist body, in 2003 that apologized for how Baptists have done little to adjust a theology that "nurtures an attitude of cultural supremacy . . . over" Muslims or to "counter the prejudice of centuries." Since 2005,

INTRODUCTION—MY PERSONAL JOURNEY

several of my books have explored many of the issues I address in this volume. What follows draws especially on two earlier books, *In Search of Muhammad* (1998) and *In Search of Jesus* (2001), and on three chapters written for a series edited by David Emmanuel Singh of the Oxford Centre for Mission Studies, *Jesus and the Cross* (2008), *Jesus and the Incarnation* (2011), and *Jesus and the Resurrection* (2013), all subtitled *Reflections of Christians from Islamic Contexts*. Kenneth Cragg was a fellow contributor. Since 2014 I have benefited from taking part in the *Christian-Muslim Relations: A Bibliographical History* project based at Birmingham University under the direction of David Thomas. The series is published by Brill. Researching, writing, and editing entries (I am a section editor and regional team leader) has extended my knowledge of how Christians have responded to Islam over the centuries, helping me draw on a tradition of finding affinity rather than expressing antipathy while attempting to remain loyal to the faith we profess.

Outline of Contents

My next chapter focuses on the person of Muḥammad, asking, "Can Christians appreciate the prophet Muḥammad as a genuine messenger from God or is this theological treason?" Chapter 2 asks how Christians might respond to the Muslim claim that Jesus was a prophet and is not God incarnate. Chapter 3 explores whether Christians can, with integrity, regard the Qur'ān as a word from God; chapter 4, whether there is any possibility of rapprochement on the issue of whether Jesus died on the cross, which Islam regards as a Christian myth. Chapter 5 traces the story of formal, church-sponsored dialogue with Muslims mainly in the United States but also by the WCC and Vatican. This provides the wider context of my personal engagement. The final chapter suggests steps that congregations or groups might take to develop empathy with Muslims against the background of popular anti-Muslim hostility and negative media coverage and to enter partnerships with them in the sphere of social engagement. I conclude with a brief afterword of final thoughts.

Chapter One

Can Christians Appreciate the Prophet Muhammad as a Genuine Messenger from God or Is This Theological Treason?

Three Responses

FROM the beginning of encounter between Christians and Muslims much debate has centered on the person of Muḥammad, whether he was sincere, a divinely commissioned prophet or a moral reprobate and fraudster. Early in my days as a student at Selly Oak, David Kerr drew my attention to how Muslim reverence for Jesus, whom the Qur'ān honors as a prophet, creates asymmetry with how Christians routinely denounce Muḥammad as an imposter or even as satanically inspired, often applying to him such biblical verses as those that denounce false prophets and false teachers. I have described this as the problem of the "too little" meeting the "too much," "Muslims (for Christians) make 'too little' of Jesus Christ, and Christians (for Muslims) make 'too much' of Him."[1] Some Christians refer to Muḥammad as the pretend or pseudo-prophet, or place "prophet" in quotation marks. In contrast, pious Muslims prefix Jesus' name with the salutation "peace be upon him." In a 1984 article, Kerr pointed out that "few Christians have been able to reply affirmatively to the age-old Muslim question, 'Since we [Muslims] accept Jesus as a genuine prophet and messenger of God, can you [Christians] not reciprocate by accepting the genuineness of Muhamamd's prophethood?'"[2] Also in 1984, Kenneth Cragg cited a Muslim participant at a 1975 dialogue meeting in Libya: "There is an issue that disturbs Muslims more than any other in their approach to Christians

---

1. Bennett, "Theological Appreciation", 249.
2. Kerr, "Prophet Muhammad," 112.

... it is the silence and reserve of Christians regarding Muḥammad" (viii). Kerr describes this as "one of the most critical areas of Christian-Muslim debate."[3] As such, the question, "Can Christians appreciate the prophet Muḥammad as a genuine messenger from God or is this theological treason" seems appropriate for exploration in this first chapter. Ever since Muḥammad preached his message in seventh-century Arabia, the majority of Christians have had little positive to say about him. It should be said, at the outset, that many Christians continue to hold negative views of Muḥammad. The best-selling books on Muḥammad by Christians today are those written by evangelicals such as Emir Fethi Caner and Mehmet Caner for whom Muslims and Christians *do not even worship the same God.* For these Christians, there is no common ground between Christianity and Islam. Given this negativity, which persists, this chapter will identify responses that shift away from total hostility toward a more positive view of Muḥammad, that is, toward affirming that *some common ground* exists between Islam and Christianity. There is also a close correlation between what Christians think about Muḥammad and Islam, and their view of Christianity's relationship—or lack of relationship—with other religions, and with beliefs about the possibility of salvation for non-Christians. While theologically problematic, given that Muḥammad's position in Islam as God's messenger, and Jesus' position in Christianity as God incarnate, are different, discussion also tends to draw comparisons between Muḥammad and Jesus. Such comparisons feature in both early and very recent texts. Strictly speaking, the correct theological comparison would be between the Qurʾān, which is Revelation, the eternal Word, in Islam, and Jesus, who is the eternal Word in Christianity. For Muslims, God's Word became a book. For Christians, God's Word became flesh. Yet it can be argued that the Muḥammad-Jesus comparison is appropriate because it is almost impossible to talk about Muḥammad without also talking about the Qurʾān, or indeed about the Qurʾān without talking of Muḥammad. I tend to see the Prophet-Book as representing a single revelatory unit. I also agree with Cragg that "the question of a Christian acknowledgment of Muhammad resolves itself into that of a Christian response to the Islamic scripture." "Muhammad," he continues, "would not have it otherwise" adding "nor could any faithful Muslim."[4] A Christian who sees the Qurʾān as wholly Muḥammad's creation full of questionable rules and dubious content is

3. Kerr, "Prophet Muhammad," 112.
4. Cragg, *Muhammad and the Christian*, 6.

unlikely to see anything commendable in Muḥammad or to say anything positive about him. I have argued, too, that while Jesus and Muḥammad may not be theologically commensurate, they are "functionally commensurate" in terms of the place they occupy in believers' hearts.[5]

In what follows, the degree to which Christian views of Muḥammad reflect actual encounter with Muslims—or lack of encounter—is also highlighted; the *context* of Christian thinking about Muḥammad often shapes the *content* of that thought. Social, political, and international factors affect the way in which Christians regard Muslims and their Prophet. Access or lack of access to Islamic sources is another important factor behind the ways in which views develop. On the other hand, theological conviction plays a more dominant role; thus, neither encounter nor access to authentic Islamic sources necessarily results in more positive ideas about Muḥammad. Christians may choose to distrust these as unreliable or as insufficiency early. In my doctoral work, the three scholars whose work I categorized as representing a conciliatory attitude to Islam had little or no contact with Muslims or knowledge of Arabic while the three who were hostile and confrontational had experience of life in Muslim contexts and had studied Arabic. This chapter identifies three stances that characterize how Christians have responded to Muḥammad. The first response represents a denial of Muḥammad, expressing a total rejection of Islam; Muslims must convert or remain spiritually lost. This view is often accompanied by a confrontational attitude that posits a civilizational clash between Muslim-majority and non-Muslim-majority space; there is no possibility for the salvation of non-Christians. Muslims represent an unwelcome and even a dangerous presence in non-Muslim majority states to which their migration should be restricted. The second response expresses limited positivity; conversion is necessary for salvation but Christians can identify positive aspects of Muḥammad's legacy when attempting to evangelize Muslims; other religions may find fulfilment in Christian faith but are not themselves "saving." The third position moves toward a Muslim view of Muḥammad as a genuine prophet; while problematic issues remain, this position allows that Muslims may, without necessarily becoming Christian, find divine favor. Salvation is through *Christ* but not necessarily *Christianity*. The first of these responses could be described as exclusivist in terms of Race's three paradigms. The second would also qualify as exclusivist although these Christians will, in practice, relate more cordially with Muslims and modify

---

5. Bennett, *In Search of Muhammad*, 227.

what they say and write about Muḥammad. The third response qualifies as inclusivist. With respect to a pluralist position, my own thinking is that this cannot be described as a Christian view. This would involve Christians accepting everything that Muḥammad taught, which would require rejecting much of what Christians believe about Jesus or going beyond what most will affirm. In this chapter, I share Cragg's goal, in his *Muhammad and the Christian* (1984):

> It is the aim of this study to offer at least one Christian's view of a resolution of the problem, a resolution which, no more than tentative, remains loyal to Christian criteria while outlining a positive response to Muhammad.[6]

Kerr and Cragg feature below in my discussion of the third response where I also outline my attempt to resolve the problem.

The Denial of Muḥammad

Negative Christian attitudes toward Muḥammad, representing a complete denial that his life had any positive aspects, reject everything that Muslims believe to be true about his character, spiritual status, and significance. For Muslims, Muḥammad was the perfect man, whose moral conduct presents the best model to be imitated. He was incapable of sin. He was divinely commissioned as the universal prophet, the last of thousands of prophets called by God to teach the difference between godly and ungodly conduct. This message is set out in the Qurʾān which God revealed to Muḥammad through the angel Gabriel over a period of twenty-three years, between 610 and 632. The Qurʾān is God's speech, containing no humanly authored content. Earlier prophets, including Abraham, Moses, and Jesus, are honoured, as are the books that some prophets, known as apostles, also received, though Muḥammad's scripture corrects errors that over time compromised these. Thus it represents the definitive guide. Some Muslims say that salvation is only available to those who affirm both the oneness of God and the apostleship of Muḥammad. Almost point by point, these beliefs are contested, rejected, and denied by Christians, who see Muḥammad very differently. Only such facts as when and where Muḥammad was born, when he began to claim to be a prophet, where and how he died, are accepted,

---

6. Cragg, *Muhammad and the Christian*, viii.

although for centuries many of these details were unknown or twisted in various ways in Christian writing.

An early example is found in a brief Latin life of Muḥammad written in Spain in about 850 CE. The writer was living under Muslim rule, so might have consulted Muslims to find out what they believed. Given that some factually accurate information is contained in the *Life*, the author may have had access to an early Muslim source; the earliest surviving biography of Muḥammad had been written about a hundred years before. However, he was evidently predisposed to view Islam, Muslims, and Muḥammad in the darkest way possible, and calumny could still substitute for fact and negative assertions about Muḥammad replace positive Muslim beliefs. The *Life* correctly states that Muḥammad was an orphan who worked for and later married a wealthy widow. However, it quickly turns this into something sinister and odious, describing him as "aflame with the fuel of his lust."[7] Aware that Muḥammad traveled on business and encountered Christians, which Muslim sources also describe, the *Life* has it that Muḥammad attended Christian assemblies and, "as a shrewd son of darkness," committed Christian sermons to memory. Then, pretending to receive visits from the angel Gabriel, who allegedly brought him divine revelation, he presented himself as a prophet. He was swollen with pride, though it was actually a trained vulture that came to him, which the *Life* calls "the spirit of error," leaving open the possibility that this was Satan in disguise. Muḥammad preached to "irrational animals." His followers were ordered to take up arms in his name and established Damascus as their capital (though this city was not captured until 634 and became the capital only in 661). Muḥammad's lust again features in a reference to his marriage with the wife of his adopted son Zayd, which he justified by passing off a verse of his "Law" (Q 33:37, paraphrased quite accurately) "as of divine inspiration." He "arranged other songs in the honor of Joseph, Zachary and even the mother of the Lord, Mary."[8] This correctly identifies Sūras 12 and 19 by their titles. It was this sin among many that precipitated his death. Aware that "he would in no way be resurrected on his own merit," the "false prophet" ordered his followers to guard his body, anticipating a miracle. However, instead of rising after three days, his body began to give off a horrendous stench that drew dogs who devoured the corpse: in memory of this, Muslims slaughter dogs every year. A later legend situated Muḥammad's tomb at Mecca, where his

7. Wolf, "Life of Muhammad," 48.
8. Wolf, "Life of Muhammad," 49.

iron coffin was suspended in the air by a giant magnet (some others correctly locate Muḥammad's tomb at Medina).

Many of these details became standard features of this approach, namely, that Muḥammad was a sexual reprobate, pretended to be a prophet, composed the Qurʾān to advance his personal goals, practiced black magic, gained followers by force or deception, faked Gabriel's appearances, plagiarized the Bible or was influenced by Christians, committed many sins and falsely predicted his resurrection. In fact, as had John of Damascus writing about 749CE, the Latin *Life* described Muḥammad as a heresiarch, thus depicting Islam as a deviant form of Christianity. John, who had also referred to the Zayd-Zaynab affair, speculating about Muḥammad's state of mind during his supposed revelatory experiences, suggested that as Muḥammad was sleeping when "the Book came to him" we could rightly conclude that all he experienced was dreams.[9] By the eleventh century, the popular *Song of Roland* had Muslims worshipping three deities, Apollin, Tevaggon, and Mahom[10] (with the latter identified as Muḥammad). Muḥammad's illiteracy, which most Muslims affirm, has been routinely rejected by Christian authors, who usually assume without question that he wrote the Qurʾān.

Rarely were correct dates given for Muḥammad's life. The year 666 became popular, thus identifying Muḥammad with the Beast of Revelation. He was frequently referred to as the (or an) Antichrist; John calls him a *forerunner* of the Antichrist.[11] Nor was his name transliterated into European languages very accurately. Several pejorative terms entered English usage derived from his name, including "mummery" and "mawmet," meaning superstition (John called Islam a "deceptive superstition"), and possibly "miscreant" as well. Over time, Muḥammad was accused of practising black magic. An early and persistent idea was that his revelatory experiences were actually some type of seizure, such as epilepsy (referred to as "the falling sickness"), or were crazed delusions. In fact, during his own lifetime, Muḥammad's opponents called him a liar, mad, demon-possessed, or bewitched, just as they accused him of acquiring what he knew from a Christian slave called Jabr, as possibly reflected in Q 68:1–3 and 16:103.[12] An Arabic work known as the *Risālat al-Kindī*, an anonymous diatribe against Muḥammad and the Qurʾān attributed to a certain

---

9. Sahas, *John of Damascus*, 135.
10. *Song of Roland*, v. 3490, http://omacl.org/Roland/r234-291.html.
11. Sahas, *John of Damascus*, 133.
12. Ibn Isḥāq, *Life of Muhammad*, 121, 130, 180.

Christian named ʿAbd al-Masīḥ al-Kindī (almost certainly a pseudonym), probably written in Baghdad in the early ninth century, did much to perpetuate the denial of Muḥammad through translation into Latin in the thirteenth century and inclusion in the 1543 printed edition of the first Latin rendering of the Qurʾān; William Muir (one of the scholars whose work I analyzed in my doctoral thesis) produced an English abridgement in 1881. According to this, Muḥammad lacked any qualification to be considered, as Muslims claim, a "blessing and mercy to mankind." His lack of miracles, of biblical attestation (Muslims frequently cite biblical verses that they say predict Muḥammad), use of the sword, immoral conduct, sexual excesses, assassination of critics, and jumbled, contradictory message offer the world nothing of value. Muḥammad only offers sexual licence and a sensual paradise. The anonymous Christian author contrasts Jesus as Saviour with Muḥammad who cannot save, Jesus as peaceful with Muḥammad who is warlike, Jesus as predicted by the prophets of the Old Testament with Muḥammad who lacked any accreditation[13] and Jesus who performed miracles with Muḥammad whose own book denied that he could, although he cited stories of miracles, which he called "fabulous."[14] Muḥammad's denial that Jesus was crucified and that God is Triune leaves no room to see him as anything other than an opportunist and imposter.[15] His goals were all self-serving, to achieve power and indulge his sexual appetite. A tradition much cited by Christians says that he could pleasure forty women in a single night. The author hints at satanic origins as well, something about which other Christian authors have been explicit. Given how prominently a sword-wielding Muḥammad features in this view, it should be noted that Muslims reject the contention that Muḥammad forced people to convert to his faith, although they do acknowledge that Muḥammad used the sword in self-defence. None of the incidents in Muḥammad's life that Christians who deny him completely choose to censure are interpreted negatively by Muslim writers, including his multiple marriages. Muslims see these as Muḥammad's way of providing for widows or sealing important alliances, Christians regard them as sexual license. Denial literature often contrasts the warrior Muḥammad, seeing the sword as omnipresent in Islam, with Jesus as the Prince of Peace despite there being a strong case that Muḥammad

13. Muir, *Apology of Al-Kindy*, 51.
14. Muir, *Apology of Al-Kindy*, 121.
15. Muir, *Apology of Al-Kindy*, 110.

only engaged in defensive wars that meet the criteria of Christian just war theory.

Unveiling Islam (2002), written by the Caners, two Turkish brothers who describe themselves as former Muslims, is a best-selling text in the denial tradition. This book won the Evangelical Publishers Association's Gold Medallion in 2003. On the one hand, their summary of the details of Muḥammad's life in terms of chronology and events is well informed, but on the other, at every point they compare Muḥammad negatively with Jesus: thus, Jesus was perfect while Muḥammad sinned, Jesus taught forgiveness while Muḥammad taught revenge, Jesus was peaceful while Muḥammad "urged use of the sword," Jesus intercedes for humans before God but Muḥammad is no advocate.[16] Nor is Allah the God that Christians worship (207). Muḥammad "oscillated between revelations from Satan and Allah."[17] The Zayd-Zaynab affair and ʿĀʾisha's age when Muḥammad married her are highlighted as examples of Muḥammad's immoral behavior; thus his "life can be summed up in the words *complexity*, *expediency*, and *depravity*."[18] In June 2002, having read this book, the former president of the Southern Baptist Convention Jerry Vines described Muḥammad as a "demon-possessed paedophile." Repeated on radio by Jerry Falwell, who added that he thought that Muḥammad was a terrorist, this led to violent riots, the burning of churches, and several deaths. Fierce as such words sound, deliberate insulting of Muḥammad by Christians has a long history. It dates at least back as far as the martyrs of Cordoba in the ninth century, who publicly vilified Muḥammad, believing that this would hasten the apocalypse, for which they were executed. Francis of Assisi in the thirteenth century was unusual in suggesting that instead of killing Muslims, Christians might evangelize them, though contemporary members of his own order chose to insult Muḥammad outside the ruler's palace in Seville, for which they were deported. They did the same in Morocco, for which they were imprisoned. They were moved from jail to jail, perhaps in the hope that this would silence them (an indication of Muslim forbearance), though in the end they too were executed.[19] Early Franciscan missionaries in India in 1321 CE, asked by Muslims what they thought about Muḥammad, replied that he was keeping his father company in hell, where

---

16. Caner and Caner, *Unveiling Islam*, 245–46.
17. Caner and Caner, *Unveiling Islam*, 44.
18. Caner and Caner, *Unveiling Islam*, 63.
19. Daniel, *Islam and the West*, 144.

his followers would join him, for which they were beheaded.[20] It should be noted, though, that very negative comments about Muḥammad were often primarily intended for Christian consumption, to reassure them that their religion was superior to Islam. Often, even when encounter with Muslims was possible, Christians had little real contact with them. Those who lived at a distance tended to see the Muslim world as an actual or potential foe, a political or imperial rival, which obviously colored what they wrote about him.

Limited Positivity

Typically, this view of Muḥammad identifies certain aspects of his teaching or life that can be described as positive, while maintaining that Muslims are unredeemed. However, Islam may find fulfilment in Christianity, which many Christians say already fulfills Judaism. One midway position between total denial of Muḥammad and limited positivity sees God's hand behind Muḥammad's life but only as a punishment against Christian disunity. An early example of this has been attributed to the Byzantine emperor Heraclius, Muḥammad's contemporary, as recorded by Barhebraeus (d. 1286).[21] One of the first scholarly lives of Muḥammad in English that drew on early Islamic sources was the nineteenth-century scholar and colonial officer William Muir's four-volume *Life of Mahomet* (1861), which pioneered the reconstruction of the original order of the Qurʾān's chapters as a context for the biography. His final estimate of Muḥammad was emphatically negative; like the more recent Caners, he depicts Muḥammad as struggling between satanic and divine influence. However, he does portray the first phase of Muḥammad's prophetic ministry until 622 CE in positive terms as a sincere search for truth. It was only later that his ambition and personal indulgence led him into conscious fraud and a "compromise with evil."[22] For all this Muir could not but help admire aspects of Muḥammad's life, such as his loyalty to friends, his simple, unpretentious lifestyle, his urbanity, kindliness of disposition and moderation, although Muir also remarks on his cruelty toward his enemies, his perfidy, and his polygamous marriages.[23]

20. Kanjamala and Arles, *Christian Mission*, 264.
21. Bar Hebraeus, *Chronography*, 1:90.
22. Muir, *Life of Mahomet*, 2:90.
23. Muir, *Life of Mahomet*, 4:302–24.

Even so, "inconsistencies run through" his character.[24] Despite his negative assessment of Islam, Muir enjoyed warm relations with a number of notable Indian Muslims.

Others who subscribe to partial affirmation list Islam's strengths alongside its weaknesses, suggesting that the former can prepare the way for Christianity. William St. Clair Tisdall (1859–1928), a missionary in India and Iran who knew Muir, whose work I also analyzed in my doctoral thesis, thought Christians too hasty in dismissing Muslim prayer as mechanical.[25] He repeated many of the familiar criticisms leveled at Islam but argued that "no absolutely false system has ever prevailed among men,"[26] explaining that positive elements in any religion find "their completion, their fulfilment, their realization" in Christian truth.[27] However, such limited positivity does not necessarily ascribe any direct divine activity in Islam (special revelation) but may attribute these to "general" or "natural" revelations, that is, to truth about God that can be discovered from observing the physical universe, or by means of philosophical reasoning.

Lewis Bevan Jones's approach, too, represents a partially positive response. Jones's long experience in India, where he was born, convinced him that the Holy Spirit is at work within Islam and Muslims: "We should rejoice in whatever evidence we find of the presence of God's Spirit in Islam and in every witness it makes to his Being and Majesty."[28] He invited Christians to explore with Muslims the shared "phenomenon of religious experience."[29] The Spirit is at work in Muslim as well as in Christian hearts. He thought that an ill-informed and prejudicial view of Muḥammad, including seeing him as an impostor, handicapped the evangelical task. On the other hand, when he compared Muḥammad with Jesus, he could not but comment that "grave moral defects" reflect unfavorably on the former. Yet his overall aim was to penetrate beyond prejudice and polemics to Islam's inner meaning, and to the sharing of spiritual experience, to what he described as "the rarer atmosphere of the things of the spirit." He criticized much earlier Christian writing on Islam as bankrupt. This often attracted very negative Muslim responses. Even when such literature did lead to a Muslim converting, they

24. Muir, *Life of Mahomet*, 4:324.
25. Tisdall, *Religion of the Crescent*, 42.
26. Tisdall, *Christianity and Other Faiths*, 38.
27. Tisdall, *Christianity and Other Faiths*, 227.
28. Jones, *People of the Mosque*, 253.
29. Jones, *Christianity Explained*, 93.

tended to convert to what they saw as an intellectually superior faith rather than for deeply spiritual reasons.[30] In the end, Jones yearned for Muslims to become Christian. However, he succeeded in earning their respect; Muhammad Yakub Khan, imam of the Woking Mosque, wrote appreciatively of Jones's contribution in an obituary tribute.[31] Jones described his lifelong engagement with Islam as a "hard task" that involved "sacrifice, and tears, and un-requited love."[32] He was unable to glibly or quickly dismiss Islam but wrestled throughout his life with how he could understand God's presence in the lives of Muslims when their religion's teaching clashes with that of the Christian tradition.

Phil Parshall, a former SIM (Service in Mission) missionary to Bangladesh (1962–1982) and Philippines (1984–2005), a pioneer of the Messianic Muslim movement, in which converts to Christianity retain some Islamic forms, presents a partially positive evaluation in his writing. Parshall's time in Bangladesh overlapped with mine. I heard him speak once at a missionary conference in Dhaka on cultural sensitivity. Parshall completed his doctor of missiology from Fuller in 1980. Unlike many of his fellow evangelicals, Parshall says that Muslims and Christians worship the same God,[33] and rather than denying that Muslim spiritual and devotional practice has any value, he invites Christians to "equal or excel" Muslims' zeal in prayer.[34] He thinks that where possible Christians should avoid language that Muslims find offensive or objectionable, including calling Jesus God's Son, because this has carnal connotations for them.[35] He tends to endorse Muḥammad's sincerity as a God-seeker, whose ultimate fate rests with God, not with Christian critics. Morally, Muḥammad falls short of Jesus but compares favorably with Old Testament prophets.[36] Parshall does not say that Muslims as Muslims may stand in a right relationship with God, though neither does he say that everything to do with Islam has no value and must be repudiated or denied. Parshall advocates what is known as the C4 model of contextualization, in which Islamic forms considered

---

30. Jones, *People of the Mosque*, 298.
31. Bennett, "Theological Appreciation," 242.
32. Jones, *Christ's Ambassador*, 12.
33. Parshall, *Understanding Muslim Teachings*, 27.
34. Parshall, *Beyond the Mosque*, 233.
35. Parshall, *Beyond the Mosque*, 201.
36. Parshall, *Beyond the Mosque*, 260.

biblically acceptable coexist with Christian forms.³⁷ Muslim Background Believers form their own congregations. At least for Tisdall and Parshall, it seems that sustained exposure to Muslims did impact their evaluations. In several articles, though, Parshall warns that contextualization, in his view, can go too far by compromising what he sees as essential beliefs in Jesus as the only saviour and the Bible as the only word of God.³⁸

Supporters of what is called the C5 model argue that certain Islamic practices and forms can be adapted for Christian use, and that Messianic or ʿĪsā-believing Muslims may continue to act outwardly as Muslims, including praying in the mosque while believing in Jesus in their hearts. For Parshall, this "goes too far" slipping into syncretism as does referring to oneself as Muslim without any qualifier. He accepts that a Muslim convert may phase their complete severance from the Mosque to allow their faith in Christ to mature. The contextualization movement aims to avoid the problems caused by the traditional extraction method, which I described in my introduction, which leaves converts socially isolated and often far from warmly welcomed within the church whose members in Bangladesh almost all have Hindu/animist roots.

Toward a Fuller Appreciation of Muḥammad

Any Christian who wishes to remain a Christian, especially in good standing with their church or communion, will encounter problems when attempting to go beyond the partially positive view of Muḥammad. Issues such as the doctrine of the Trinity, Jesus' divine sonship, the incarnation, the reality of human sin, Jesus' death on the cross, the status of the Qurʾān and the integrity of the Bible all present serious challenges. Christians have found it easier to see a biblical verse such as Matthew 24:24, on the coming of false prophets, as pointing to Muḥammad than they have to identify biblical affirmation for his claims. To affirm of Muḥammad exactly what Muslims do might imply that one would view Jesus as they do, as well, and may also involve elevating the Qurʾān over the Bible as God's definitive disclosure to humanity.

Some writers who have shifted toward a Muslim view of Muḥammad have had issues with normative Christology, tending to affirm a Unitarian or Arian position. The former see Jesus as an ordinary but morally and

---

37. On these models, see Travis, "C1 to C6 Spectrum."
38. See Parshall, "Danger!" and "Going Too Far?"

spiritually exemplary man. The latter see Jesus as Christ as created in time by God to whom he is subordinate not coeternal and coequal. One of the first non-Muslims to write almost entirely positively about Muḥammad was the English author Henry Stubbe (1632–1676), who wrote *An account of the rise and progress of Mahometanism, and a vindication of Mahomet and his religion from the calumnies of the Christians* around 1674. This remained in manuscript until 1911 when it was first published by a Muslim, Hafiz Mahmud Khan Shairani, who praised its "importance as the earliest known sympathetic composition in English literature."[39] Stubbe did not have personal contact with Muslims or knowledge of Arabic but he did pioneer the realization that sources which were "indigenous to Islamic civilization could lead to a new understanding of contested history and a reassessment of the most misrepresented man in early modern European religious thought."[40] Stubbe subscribed formally to the doctrines of the Church of England but thought the Trinity ridiculous. Transliterating Muḥammad's name correctly, he castigated others for misspelling this and for reading all sorts of malignant notions into their versions.[41] Dismissing calumny after calumny made by earlier Christians as unfounded and false, including that Muḥammad's lineage was base and that he spread Islam by violence, he presented a pioneer account of Muḥammad's life that closely followed Muslim sources. He saw Muḥammad as a wise legislator whom Christians had transformed into "the vilest imposter."[42] Challenging the charge that Muḥammad suffered from epilepsy, he found nothing in accounts of Muḥammad's inspiration or revelatory visions that justified this. They were probably rather "ecstasies" similar to those experienced by "the old prophets and Paul."[43] As late as 1851, the Orientalist Aloys Sprenger (1813–1893) was arguing that at times Muḥammad was "a complete maniac," suffering from "cataleptic insanity" that produced hallucinations without loss of consciousness. This condition, *hysteria muscularis*, gave Muḥammad the propensity to lie and deceive.[44] Sprenger, who was also a medical doctor, was for some time head of the British-funded Calcutta Madrasa.

39. Shairani, *Account of the Rise*, v.
40. Matar, *Henry Stubbe*, 2.
41. Matar, *Henry Stubbe*, 189.
42. Matar, *Henry Stubbe*, 192.
43. Matar, *Henry Stubbe*, 127; on Stubbe, see Bennett, "Henry Stubbe."
44. Sprenger, *Life of Mohamed*, 6:114–16, *Das Leben*, I: 207.

Stubbe's position does not represent one that a Trinitarian Christian can easily adopt and may be closer to the humanist view of Edward Gibbon (1737–1794). In what he wrote on Muḥammad, Gibbon expressed admiration for a creed that was free from dogmas and priests (as he saw it) and that offered a straightforward, rational message that still motivated women and men. It had taken great courage for Muḥammad to achieve what he did, unifying a divided Arabia. Christians had distorted Jesus' teachings, while Muslims maintain the purity and simplicity of Muḥammad's. Gibbon dismissed as absurd the myth about Muḥammad's tomb being suspended in midair in Mecca.[45] For Gibbon, Muḥammad was a gifted legislator rather than a divinely commissioned messenger. For a while, I was tempted to abandon a Trinitarian faith, writing about this in a 1981 article and even contemplated transferring to the Unitarian ministry.[46] However, I found ways of personally reconciling belief in God's Oneness and in the Trinity, mainly derived from Jones's writing, who stressed that Trinity is rooted in the Christian experience of God's revelation from which they inferred God's Triune nature, "God as Father" as "proclaimed by Jesus, Jesus Himself . . . and the Holy Spirit at work in them" yet which are "essentially ONE in redemptive purpose and activity."[47] I have remained a Trinity affirming Christian.

Swedish bishop Tor Andrae (1885–1947) offered an important reevaluation of Muḥammad in *Muhammad: The Man and His Faith* (1936), in which he located Muḥammad's revelatory episodes within a general framework of mystical experience, comparing him with shamans.[48] Andrae accepted Muḥammad's sincerity and the genuineness of his religious experience,[49] and unlike Muir he saw more continuity between the pre- and post-*hijra* phases of Muḥammad's life. The latter period gave him the opportunity to put his political ideas into practice, but his aim was always spiritual as well as political, to set up a "religious community" that was also political in character.[50] Andrae did criticize certain actions of Muḥammad as moral lapses but also made an effort to understand why he acted as he did. For example, his alleged killing of a poet was because the vilifications

45. Gibbon, *Decline and Fall*, 5:248n151.
46. Bennett, "Flirtation with Unitarianism."
47. Jones, *Christianity Explained*, 92.
48. Andrae, *Muhammad the Man*, 59.
49. Andrae, *Muhammad the Man*, 62–64, 233.
50. Andrae, *Muhammad the Man*, 86.

circulated by this opponent posed a serious threat to Muḥammad's esteem among his contemporaries, on which he heavily depended.[51]

Notwithstanding the challenges and difficulties involved in offering positive statements about Muḥammad while retaining Christian integrity, perhaps the first ever attempt was offered at a very early date by the Nestorian Patriarch Timothy II (d. 823) in conversation with the ʿAbbasid Caliph al-Mahdī (d. 785). When on the second day of exchanges al-Mahdī asked him what he thought of Muḥammad, Timothy replied:

> Muḥammad is worthy of all praise, by all reasonable people, O my Sovereign. He walked in the path of the prophets, and trod in the track of the lovers of God. All the prophets taught the doctrine of one God, and since Muḥammad taught the doctrine of the unity of God, he walked, therefore, in the path of the prophets.

He took people "nearer to good works," opposed "idolatry," taught "knowledge of one God" and about "God, His Word and His Spirit."[52]

On the one hand, this statement leaves a lot of questions unanswered, including what exactly Timothy meant by Muḥammad walking in the path of the prophets (see Samir, *Prophet Muḥammad*, for a less positive interpretation of these words of Timothy). The rest of the exchange makes it clear that he did not alter his stance on the Trinity, Jesus' incarnation or death, or Muḥammad's lack of biblical attestation, even though the caliph cited the allusions in John's gospel to the coming of the Paraclete as evidence of this, which is one of the earliest references to Muslim identification of the Paraclete with Muḥammad rather than with the Holy Spirit as Christians understand John 14:16. Muslims point to quite a few Bible verses as predictive of Muḥammad. However, rather as Jews do not see Jesus in verses that Christians cite as pointing to him in their turn Christians do not recognize Muḥammad in those verses that Muslims cite. Timothy enjoyed a very cordial relationship with al-Mahdī, which would have influenced his approach to Islam. David Kerr suggested that Timothy and his Nestorian church were much less "constricted by the Mediterranean power politics of their coreligionists in the West and could accept Muhammad as being unquestionably 'in the way of the prophets.'"[53] They saw the Spirit of God as universally active in human life, an emphasis also found in the writing of Orthodox bishop George Khodr, whose view Kerr summarized. For Khodr, the Spirit

---

51. Andrae, *Muhammad the Man*, 207.
52. Mingana, *Apology of Timothy*, 16.
53. Kerr, "Prophet Muhammad," 115.

"links all humankind with the eternity transcending history, as signalled in the economy of Christ—the universal sign that all humans are made participants in the creative and salvific activity of God."[54] Timothy may be close to Henry Stubbe and, more recently, to Cragg and even Parshall in comparing Muḥammad to Hebrew prophets in terms of his God-inspired activities.

Reginald Bosworth Smith (1839–1908), biographer, historian, and Harrow house master, whose writing attracted Muslim approval, also believed that Christians should regard Muḥammad as a genuine prophet. Interestingly, Muslims often describe Smith as a missionary (he was not) and add "Reverend" to his name. He was actually an active Anglican Lay Christian. Possibly, his lay status afforded him more freedom to think about Muḥammad in ways that an ordained person might hesitate to do as Matar suggests was true of Henry Stubbe.[55] I analyzed Smith's work in my doctoral thesis and admire his contribution. He proposed what I have called a historical key to understand Muḥammad. Smith's *Mohammed and Mahammedenism* was first published in 1874. Smith criticized earlier writers for writing "to prove a thesis"—Muḥammad was either to be "a Hero or an imposer."[56] Consequently, he says, we learn much that has been said about Muḥammad but comparatively little of Muḥammad himself. Christians often fail to shine the light on their own bad conduct while choosing to highlight Muslim failures to meet Islam's highest demands which they confuse with Islam per se.[57] While acknowledging "paramount allegiance to Christianity," Smith attempted to penetrate behind the historical records to the facts they describe, believing that God should not be "localized exclusively in one place or creed" but traced "everywhere in measure." Inspiration in the "broadest sense of the word," he believed, was "found everywhere in all the greatest thoughts of men, for the workings of God are everywhere, and the spirits of men and nations are moulded by Him to bring about his purposes of love."[58] Smith believed in the ultimate triumph of God's love. Smith wrote of "that . . . unity above and beyond [the] unity of Christendom which, properly understood, all earnest Christians so much desire; a unity which rests upon the belief that the children of the one Father may worship

---

54. Khodr, "Economy of the Spirit," 115.
55. Matar, *Henry Stubbe*, 46.
56. Smith, *Mohammed and Mohammedenism*, 83.
57. Smith, *Mohammed and Mohammedenism*, xii.
58. Smith, *Mohammed and Mohammedenism*, xvi.

Him under different names: that they may be influenced by one spirit, even though they know it not, they may all have one hope, even if they have not one faith."[59] He called for a process of "mutual approximation and . . . understanding" through which Christianity and Islam might become allies in the task of spreading the recognition of God's sovereignty and the call to live according to God's will.

Smith argued in favor of Islam's civilizing role. He saw Islam as an ally. Influenced by evolutionary thinking, he tended to regard Islam as suitable for Africa and Asia, and Christianity as suitable for Europeans which may be similar to how Paul of Antioch and more recently Kerr acknowledge Muḥammad as the prophet for Arabs. However, he also questioned Europe's assumption of racial and cultural superiority and suggested that Christian missionaries could learn much from the example of their Muslim counterparts, who "showed forbearance and a sympathy for native customs and prejudices and even for their harmless beliefs." Smith explicitly rejected Muir's verdict that Muḥammad was guilty of imposture and that a moral decline occurred after the *Hijra* (migration from Mecca to Medina in 620 CE). Instead, a substantial unity can be traced through each stage of Muḥammad's life.[60] From first until last, Muḥammad claimed "that title only with which he had begun, and which the highest philosophy and the truest Christianity will one day, I venture to believe, agree in yielding to him—that of a prophet, a very prophet of God."[61] Smith attracted the gratitude, friendship, and appreciation of some Muslims. One of these Muslims, Sayyid Amir Alī (1849–1928) called Muir "an avowed enemy of Islam"[62] but praised Smith. He wrote, "Your book has not only confirmed me in my own faith but it has given me as far higher opinion of Christianity than I yet expressed."[63] On the one hand, Smith fell short of explaining how Christians might yield to Muḥammad the title of prophet expressing this hope in aspirational not propositional terms. On the other hand, by accommodating him within a revelatory framework of God's universal activity, even though this is probably still "too little" for Muslims, his work went beyond Christian denial of Muḥammad.

---

59. Smith, *Mohammed and Mohammedenism*, xxv–xxvi.
60. Smith, *Mohammed and Mohammedenism*, 141.
61. Smith, *Mohammed and Mohammedenism*, 344.
62. ʿAlī, *Spirit of Islam*, 104.
63. Grogan, *Reginald Bosworth Smith*, 148.

IN SEARCH OF UNDERSTANDING

David Kerr's contribution to a Christian reevaluation of Muḥammad was inspired by Timothy whose work he first drew to my attention. Timothy's *Apology* was unknown in the West until Alphonse Mingana produced an English translation in 1928 but it was widely circulated in the Arab world. In his 1984 paper, one of several that Kerr wrote on Christian response to Muḥammad, he offers six considerations on which a contemporary Christian theological response to the question, "Do you accept Muhammad as a prophet" might be formulated. These are:

1. God's revelation of his word as the power over, within, and beyond creation is universal, and is universally performative of his purposes in achieving what the Bible terms "the kingdom of God" (which in meaning is by no means strange to the vision of the Qurʾān).

2. Divine revelation is evidenced universally in nature and in human history, through communities and individuals, and in the deepest apprehensions of the religious traditions that have evolved around them.

3. The Bible, in its Hebrew and Greek parts, provides us with a centuries-long set of interpretations of divine revelation through the graphic record of God's actions in the history of Israel, exemplifying the universal pattern of divine activity in the analysis of a particular people and, in the New Testament, a particular person, Jesus, and the apostolic church.

4. The gospel in Christ, for the Christian, signifies the performative pattern of universal divine revelation of which the church is called to be the doxological sign in the world, pointing however wretchedly in its history to the ontological dynamics of the kingdom of God.

5. As God has left no people without witnesses to his divine revelation, so the church in the power of the Holy Spirit should explore the many extrabiblical testimonies positively and with imagination, searching them for complementary signs of the mystery of divine providence and critically adopting them into its own doxology.

6. Muḥammad is manifestly such a sign "in the way of the prophets," the Qurʾān witnessing to the universality of divine revelation, reiterating many of the fundamental perceptions of the Bible, and providing as it were a critical commentary on the more dogmatic aspects of particularly New Testament belief, and Muḥammad exemplifying the application of the Qurʾānic vision in society.

Commenting on Kerr's view of Muḥammad, Mehmet Aydin (2002) wrote, "What Kerr indicates by this evaluation is that Christians can regard Muhammad as a witness to God's universal revelation which was revealed in Jesus Christ for all humankind and not more than that,"[64] suggesting that even when a Christian attempts to go beyond what most fellow Christians have said about Muḥammad this remains "too little" for Muslims. In one of his later essays on Muḥammad, Kerr suggests that, using a framework supplied by liberation theology, Muḥammad could be seen as a prophet sent by God specifically for the Arab world. As Hebrew prophets were tasked with liberating the Israelites, so Muḥammad's task was to liberate Arabs. Liberation theology stresses God's specific concern for the just ordering of society, which is expressed as the preferential option for the poor.[65] Drawing on the work of Christian thinkers, Farid Esack has articulated an Islamic theology of liberation which highlights the Qur'ān's empathy with the oppressed, and its demand for the just and equitable ordering of human society.[66] For some Christians and Muslims, liberation theology, like the social gospel, is overly focused on this world and too little on spiritual redemption. Yet, in both Bible and Qur'ān, God's demand for justice is so explicit that it is difficult to see how failing to work toward achieving this could be described as pleasing to God. We might ask whether God would prefer to hear Muslims and Christian argue endlessly about their doctrines or feed the hungry and house the homeless.

Affirming Muḥammad as the Arab prophet probably dates from the writing of Paul of Antioch, a Melkite bishop in Lebanon. Paul wrote "Letter to a Muslim Friend" around about 1200 CE.[67] This brief text (24 pp.) was later revised and expanded as "The Letter from the People of Cyprus" and sent to the Muslim scholar Ibn Taymiyya in 1316 (and to another well-known Muslim). Both texts represent Islam as a valid faith for Arabs and Muḥammad as a legitimate prophet for the people to whom he had been sent but contend that Christians were not among those people. Paul wrote that Muḥammad was sent to the "ignorant Arabs" but that there is "no obligation for us to follow him," Christians had already received their

---

64. Aydin, *Modern Western*, 195.

65. See Kerr, "Muhammad: Prophet of Liberation."

66. See Esack, *Qur'an, Liberation & Pluralism*.

67. See translation at https://www.researchgate.net/publication/268216125_Paul%27s_Letter_to_the_Muslims_English_Translation_from_Arabic_and_French_source_documents.

messenger who had spoken to them in their own languages. God sends different messengers to different nations (Q5:44). When the Qurʾān says that God will accept no other religion (*dīn*) than Islam (Q3:85) it refers to the people to whom God had sent Muḥammad. Referring to the Qurʾān's great praise for Mary and for Jesus, Paul also commended the verse that defends churches from attack (Q22:40), the injunctions to believe in all the Books that God has sent (42:15) and that People of the Book should not argue with each other because they share the same goal. Paul's unambiguous recognition of Muḥammad as a prophet went further than Timothy's view that Muḥammad had "walked in the path of the prophets." However, as David Thomas remarks, Paul's "gesture towards reconciliation with Islam" turned its prophet "into a local preacher who may be authentic," but whose mission was limited to the Arabs to whom he preached "an initial form of monotheism" that still fell short of "the full Trinitarian form."[68] This infuriated Ibn Taymiyya. His response emphatically called for belief in Muḥammad as the universal prophet necessary for salvation. When Christians claimed that the Qurʾān affirms their salvation at 5:82 and elsewhere this referred to Christians from before Muḥammad's time not to those who lived after his death who must accept his prophethood to have any hope of salvation. On the one hand, a limited affirmation of Muḥammad's prophetic mission might be as close as a Christian can go without denying their own faith. On the other hand, this goes beyond many more positive evaluations of Muḥammad by specifically affirming that he was a divinely commissioned prophet rather than explaining anything of value in Islam or in Muḥammad's life in terms of natural revelation. On Paul's letter and Ibn Taymīyya's response, see Ibn-Taymīyya and T. F. Michel, *A Muslim Theologian's Response to Christianity* (1984). Michel, a Jesuit priest, was a fellow drafter of the WCC document, *Issues in Christian-Muslim Relations*.

Cragg also tends to see Muḥammad's articulation of the Qurʾān as similar to the utterances of a poet rather than as God's direct speech, or indeed as similar to the speech of an Old Testament prophet. Even so, the Qurʾān may still represent divine communication. It is both a word from God and Muḥammad's words, since "despite itself" Islam "finds place for categories of relationship between divine ends and human means."[69] Muḥammad, he says, is the "Prophet of the Qurʾān,"[70] which Mahmut

68. Thomas, "Paul of Antioch," 81.
69. Cragg, *Muhammad and the Christian*, 65.
70. Cragg, *Muhammad and the Christian*, 91.

Aydin describes as "less generous" than Cragg intends because Muslims "do not recognize Muhammad only as 'the prophet of the Qurʾān' but as *Rasul Allah*, the messenger of God . . . not just a prophet for the Arabs but a prophet with a universal message for all human beings."[71] Aydin sees both Kerr and Cragg as innovative in their thinking on Muḥammad but as privileging their Christian framework while simultaneously trying to "appease Muslims."[72] Personally, I do not think that either were motivated by a desire to appease Muslims but sincerely wanted to do justice to Muḥammad without committing an act of Christian treason. Aydin, though, says that for Cragg Muḥammad's "ultimate significance points beyond himself to the ministry of Jesus Christ" (186). While Cragg refers to Muḥammad as prophet, Aydin thinks that this may be as much due to cultural sensitivity dating from when he worked in the Arab world.[73] Nonetheless, arguably Cragg went further than an expression of limited positivity in what he said about Muḥammad.

Turning to my personal attempt to articulate how a Christian might affirm Muḥammad in more positive terms, I began to reflect on this challenge after hearing Kerr speak on "Divine Revelation and the Person of the Prophet" in Toronto in April 1989. Subsequently, I wrote *In Search of Muhammad* (1998), followed by several papers and book chapters. In these, I argue that accepting paradox might be vital to any understanding of God's nature. God, who is ultimately beyond any numerical value, is both One and Triune yet also neither of these. Thus, unity and Trinity may both be equally true about God's nature,[74] although neither may represent the whole truth. This draws on Jones's suggestion that it is unnecessary to insist on doctrinal purity since no one contends that belief in the Trinity is itself "adequate to the ultimate truth about God,"[75] and that while God is revealed in Jesus, this does not exhaust revelation or prevent God from revelatory activity elsewhere. Jones observed that "our faith holds fast to contradictories—God is known, and yet not known" because before Christ

---

71. Aydin, *Modern Western*, 187.
72. Aydin, *Modern Western*, 187.
73. Aydin, *Modern Western*, 182.
74. Bennett, *In Search of Muhammad*, 234.
75. Jones, *Christianity Explained*, 95.

we stand "face to face with a profound mystery."[76] Everything we say about God is limited by the "very poverty of human language."[77]

I have suggested that God's word might both become incarnate as a person, Christ, and as a book, the Qurʾān, regarding the "how" of both to be a mystery, just as God's nature is mysterious.[78] How either the "bookification" or the incarnation of God's word happened remains a mystery. Muḥammad's life as a husband, as a political and military leader and his explicit advice related to social equality may in fact supplement the more purely spiritual guidance found in Jesus' life and teachings. Thus, acting as what Hans Küng calls a "prophetic corrective," Muḥammad reminds Christians that God, not ideas about God, must be at the center of a life of faith and that "orthodoxy and orthopraxis belong together everywhere, including politics."[79] This resonates with Kerr and Esack on the social justice and liberational imperative of obedience to the divine will. As Andrae says, Muḥammad saw the spiritual and the social as inseparable. The goals of this world, as well as those of the next, are crucial. The struggle to feed the hungry, house the homeless, end war and uphold justice is as important as correct belief. Muḥammad's passion for justice, equality and social solidarity, attested by the Qurʾān and Ḥadīth, can be meaningful for Christians without compromising Jesus' role as their definitive gauge "of any claim to represent the will of God."[80] Looking primarily to Jesus for spiritual nourishment while simultaneously looking to Muḥammad for more explicit guidance in the equally important social sphere refuses to elevate either Muhḥammad or Jesus above the other. Jesus' life for Christian remains paradigmatic of the life of love, generosity and sacrifice that God invites us to imitate while recognizing that translating this into practice requires additional advice to Jesus general injunctions to love our neighbors and to go the extra mile. Calling on employers to pay employees enough for them to enjoy a comparable life style to theirs (which reduces wealth inequality) or confiscating vacant buildings to house the homeless, derived from Muḥammad's sayings are but two examples of his guidance. He continually challenged the elite in Arabia for their corruption and ill treatment of the poor. I see biblical support for the view that God continues to guide us in

---

76. Jones, *Christianity Explained*, 76.
77. Jones, *Christianity Explained*, 94.
78. Bennett, *In Search of Muhammad*, 236.
79. Küng, *Christianity and World Religions*, 129.
80. Bennett, *In Search of Muhammad*, 235.

a verse such as John 16:13. Few Christians would want to reject the life of Francis of Assisi as offering fresh insight into the meaning of Christian discipleship. I do not hesitate to see lessons in the life of Muḥammad, either, or in that of Mahatma Gandhi. I discuss the role of Christian saints in chapter 3. Askari, writing about Jesus, says that Christians should listen to how Muslims view him and vice versa or each will be the poorer. "Islam," he wrote,

> has a mission for Christianity: reminding Christians that God transcends both number and image. And Christians have a mission to Muslims: reminding Muslims that even a strict monotheist could be self-righteous. Both Christianity and Islam will become arrogant if they do not listen to each other's critical witness.[81]

What Christians and Muslims say about Jesus, says Askari, is like two rivers which "cross different lands" and are "different from each other" but which, as they near the journey's end, merge in the ocean in which their differences are lost. "So we have a choice, we can refuse to engage in the common life that we share, or we can learn from it and move towards the ocean" as fellow seekers.[82] This complements my view that Christians should listen to God's voice speaking to us through Muḥammad lest in refusing to do so we shut out words that supplement and help to explain those of Jesus.

Finally, on Muḥammad, I argue that regarding him primarily as a social exemplar does not preclude also seeing his life as an example of spiritual health, a role he fulfills for most Muslims. Often, too, Christians neglect the regard Muslims have for Muḥammad seen especially in popular forms of devotion. Here, Constance Padwick's *Muslim Devotions* (1961) is to be recommended. She collected prayer manuals from throughout the Muslim world in which the *tasliya* features prominently, the calling down of God's blessings on Muḥammad and on his family (which also ends the rite of *salat*). Muslims dream about Muḥammad. They look to his example in all aspects of life because they revere him as the best of men (*al-Insān al-Kāmil*). His example is to be imitated (*imitatio Muhammadi*).

---

81. Askari, "Jesus in Islam," 143.
82. Askari, "Jesus in Islam," 146.

Conclusion: Is This Treason for Christians?

The specific question whether this compromises the role played by Jesus' death in the salvific process and therefore qualifies as theological treason for Christians will be discussed in chapter 4. However, the question here is whether it would be treason for Christians to call Muḥammad a prophet? Kerr ended his 1984 paper by arguing in favor of Christians also saluting Muḥammad with the *taslya*:

> Along these lines may not the Christian with integrity join with the Muslim in responding to the Qur'an's invitation to "ask blessings upon him [Muhammad] and salute him with a worthy salutation" (Q. 33:56) in the spirit of Jesus' own command: "Let there be no limit to your salutation as your heavenly Father's goodness knows no bounds" (cf. Mt. 5:48, RSV and NEB). Such salutation commits us, however, to work together as Christians and Muslims, together with all other human respondents to the universal divine revelation, for the fuller realization of God's rule on earth. It is not a concession to the dogmatic postulates of a particular religious tradition, nor is it to surrender one inadequate, chronological understanding of "finality" in revelation for another. Rather, it is to participate creatively in the universal activity of God, which challenges us to relive the experience of all the prophets, particularly Moses, Jesus, and Muhammad as they wrestled with the task of "creating peace in the city."[83]

For some Christians, to speak with any degree of sympathy about Muḥammad is tantamount to heresy. However, I argue that to see him as a man who was sincerely open to God's prompting, inspiration, and guidance, who led his followers out of idolatry into a disciplined life of monotheistic worship, encouraged them to become conscious of God in all spheres of life, who demanded social justice and the end of political corruption, may legitimately be seen as a genuine servant of God in terms of the biblical office of the prophet. While Christians have been reluctant to apply this title to anyone in the post-Christian era, viewing Jesus as the end of prophecy rather as Muslims view Muḥammad, this remains available as an office in the New Testament (see Eph 4:11). Kerr's reference to "the finality of revelation" points to Christian-Muslim rivalry on whether Jesus or Muḥammad represents the end of divine revelation. This lies at the core of the problem. If revelation ended with Jesus, Muhḥammad cannot

---

83. Kerr, "Prophet Muhammad," 115.

have received special revelation although he might have deduced truths from general revelation. If Muḥammad received the final revelation, God's Word to Muḥammad can be seen as enjoying priority over God's word in Jesus Christ. This may challenge both Muslim and Christian belief but God, who is unbound by human concepts, is still capable of self-disclosure today thus the claim of both traditions to possess the "final revelation" is dubious. At the very least, when we as Christians talk about Muḥammad we are obliged by the biblical mandate not to bear false witness against him by making false statements, and, as Paul exhorts us at Philippians 4:8, to think about everything we encounter that is honest, just, lovely, virtuous, and of "good report":

> Whatsoever things are true, whatsoever things are honest, whatsoever things are just, whatsoever things are pure, whatsoever things are lovely, whatsoever things are of good report, if there be any virtue, and if there be any praise, think on these things. (KJV)

Chapter Two

How Might Christians Respond to the Muslim Claim That Jesus Was a Prophet and Is Not God Incarnate?

Muslim and Christian Saints

This second chapter asks whether similarities exist between the role of Muslim and Christian saints that might aid us in responding to the challenge presented by the Muslim claim that Jesus is a prophet but not the Son of God, God incarnate, or the Second Person of a Trinity. I suggest that the status of sainthood in both traditions represents successful journeys along paths pioneered respectively by Muḥammad and Jesus. The lives of saints who, following Jesus' path or Muḥammad's, shone with God's presence and goodness, indicate that we also can experience what they experienced, intimacy with God, the alignment of our will with God's. Intimacy with God can never be fully articulated, so it has been taken as blasphemy. Arguably, the claim that Ṣūfī saints experience "oneness" with God or a "divine indwelling" (*ḥulūl*) and that Jesus was "one" with God are both true. However, this language is a metaphorical attempt to describe a spiritual experience that transcends our finite natures. When we elevate doctrines or formulations above experience, we lift the human above the divine. When Christians and Muslims admit that their language is limited, rapprochement on what appears to divide us—that the human and the divine can unite—becomes a possibility. More so than in chapter 1, which mainly drew on my academic work and writing, I use my exposure to Bangladeshi Islam as background for this exercise in comparative theology.

The Limit of Language

As did chapter 1, this chapter owes a considerable debt to the work of Lewis Bevan Jones, with whose conciliatory approach to Islam I have identified since I discovered his writing in Selly Oak during 1978. He had spent a good part of his career in what is now Bangladesh. I have visited the Reading Room he founded in Old Dhaka, and the nearby former Student Hostel he ran for many years. Jones recommends that, in our evangelical encounter with Muslims, we should emphasize the "why" rather than the "what" of belief. He contends that beliefs and doctrines are essentially post-experiential attempts to describe, within the poverty and limitations of human language, what people believe to be true about their experience of God. Convinced that Muslim as well as Christian religious experience is genuine, he identifies this as common ground.[1] Immediately before this remark, Jones refers to the "very real belief" among Muslims, especially among Ṣūfīs, in God's intimate dealings with people, adding that some Ṣūfīs "carried their doctrine of 'union' with the Beloved to such extravagant lengths that many of them, in days gone by, paid for their temerity with their lives." In this chapter, my exploration of the concepts of sainthood and of divine "indwelling" in Christianity and in Islam draws on Jones's suggestion that the language we use to describe divine-human encounter always fails to expresses the total truth of what we have experienced. Rather, our language attempts to articulate what can never be comprehensively described. I personally contend that both Christian and Muslim formulations may be wholly true in what they say of God and of the divine-human relationship but that we cannot claim that they express the whole truth about God. Something similar is found in the writing of al-Ghazālī (1058–1111), the great Ṣūfī mystic and Muslim theologian. In asking whether there is any common ground that can reduce the Christian-Muslim divide on Jesus as God-incarnate, the subject of this chapter, I am interested to see if admitting that our language is limited helps or hinders rapprochement on this issue. The Qur'ān depicts Jesus as a prophet who pointed people toward God but made no claim to either divinity or to being the Second Person of the Trinity. In holding these beliefs, Muslims accuse Christians of exaggerating Jesus' status. Christians make "too much" of Jesus. On Jesus' work of healing and feeding the hungry, though, the Qur'ān overlaps with the New Testament. For what the Qur'ān says about Jesus, see Geoffrey Parrinder,

---

1. Jones, *Christianity Explained*, 93.

Jesus in the Qur'an (1965 and subsequent reprints) and chapter 2 of my *Understanding Christian-Muslim Relation* (2008).

Building on Jones, I suggest that some of the distance between us when discussing Jesus as God incarnate may be reduced if we admit the genuineness of each other's *taqwā* (God-consciousness) and that the theological language we use is indicative and provisional, not definitive. On the one hand, differences in the language we use may construct barriers if one side claims that their language is accurate, correct and exhaustive. In this view, the other side is wrong, misguided or heretical. On the other hand, recognition that language has limitations when applied to the divine-human encounter may build bridges. During over a quarter of a century of involvement in Christian-Muslim encounter, I have tried to combine a scholarly contribution with pragmatic engagement in bridge-building, assisting Muslim communities in practical ways such as helping with grant applications, obtaining charitable status, and planning permission and even distributing prizes as chief guest at a Qur'ānic school. In what follows, I attempt to ground my reflections on Sainthood in Christianity and Islam as potentially helping Muslims to understand what Christians mean by "incarnation" in actual experience of encounter. I begin with an account of how encounter with Bangladeshi Islam alerted me to the possibility that "sainthood" might be a fruitful area to explore. Next, I shift to a discussion of "sainthood" in Islam (*walayat*) and Christianity as a bridge to understanding "incarnation."

Encountering Bangladeshi Islam

Although as described in my introduction I spent a relatively short period in Bangladesh (1979–1982), I have enjoyed sustained contact with Bangladeshis ever since. This included living for ten years in a Bangladeshi-majority neighborhood of Birmingham (1982–1992), where I engaged in community development activities and three subsequent visits to Bangladesh. In all these years, in conversation with Bangladeshi Muslims, many of them Ṣūfī, the issues that have most frequently surfaced surround the person of Jesus, whether as God incarnate, God's son, or the Second Person of the Trinity. In no few conversations, my Muslim acquaintance has commented that he cannot comprehend how I can claim belief in One God while insisting on calling God "triune." You call Jesus "God's son" but God "neither begets nor is begotten" (Q112:3). God could not, they insist, stoop to being born as a baby. Yet my Bangladeshi Muslim acquaintances, unlike some other Muslims whom I know, have never suggested that I am "lost" because I believe that God was present in the life and work of Jesus of Nazareth. Nor, unlike some Muslims, have they ever implied that belief in Jesus' incarnation means that I think of Mary as God's wife, or that God had sex with her. Often, after identifying the difference between their belief in Unity and my belief in Trinity and expressing puzzlement as to my belief in the latter, they assert that, despite this, we believe in the same God, implying an affirmation of Q 29:46, "dispute not with the people of the book . . . but . . . say 'we believe in the revelation that came down to you and in the revelation that came down to us, your God and our God is One and it is to Him that we bow.'" I may and probably am flattering myself, since I am well aware of my shortcomings, yet my gut feeling tells me that my Bangladeshi Muslim friends, many of whom have known me and worked with me for years without ever casting any aspersions on my spiritual well-being, think that despite my flaws my life is centered on God and my labors on their behalf to improve community welfare are nurtured by my relationship with God. My gut tells me that the genuineness of my religious experience is not at issue, even though my theological formulations may be problematic. This is different from experiences I have had with other Muslims, who make it quite clear that if I do not embrace Islam my spiritual state is suspect and my eternal destiny gravely at risk. I recall attending a Muslim Students' Association meeting on campus at SUNY New Paltz which, advertised as an interfaith meeting, was really a call to Islam. Speakers said that only Muslims are certain of pleasing God.

My observations of Bangladeshi Islam suggests to me that religious experience is center stage for many Bangladeshis, more important than dogma. My instinct is that they do not think that God saves or condemns people for the way they express theological convictions, that this is secondary to developing genuine God-consciousness, which is not contingent on "orthodox" belief. Prayer, fasting, and obligatory external acts of piety are important for Bangladeshi Muslims but inner renewal is even more important. Hence, the popularity of the *Tablīghī Jamāʿat* among Bangladeshis: this movement stresses spiritual growth, peace, and tolerance. The annual meeting outside Bangladesh's capital attracts the second-largest gathering of Muslims in the world after the *hajj*. With its Deobandi, conservative roots, *Tablīghī* has an anti-Ṣūfī stance vis-à-vis the role of saints and visits to shrines, but most Bangladeshi Muslims have Ṣūfī tendencies, even if they belong to a movement or organization that officially disapproves of Ṣūfism. *Tablīghī*'s founder, Muḥammad Ilyas (1885–1944), graduated from Deoband but was also a member of the Chistī order of *Ṣūfīs*, at least before he started the movement.² I first became aware of Ilyas, as I mentioned in my introduction, during fieldwork in Birmingham in 1979 among the Bangladeshi community when I was interested in assessing how popular Ṣūfism remains in Bangladesh aware that Bangladesh was mainly evangelized by Ṣūfīs. One writer actually confuses the *Tablīghī* gathering with a Ṣūfī convention; "Sufis in Bangladesh organize a huge Muslim gathering annually just outside Dhakka," he writes, adding that "it is second in size only to the *hajj* in Mecca."³ Given the popularity of Ṣūfism in Bangladesh, it is easy to see how anyone might assume that such a large gathering would of necessity be Ṣūfī. He is correct, though, to describe Bangladeshi Islam as tolerant "of other religions" and Bangladeshi Muslims as emphasizing "abstinence and self-denial." Uddin says that it is impossible to estimate the number of Bangladeshis who identify with Ṣūfī orders any more than it is how many belong to *Tablīghī* or to *Jamaat-e-Islam* (the main Islamist organization in Bangladesh which has had some electoral success) "as the level of association with these institutions and with Pīrs varies with each devotee." "Nevertheless," she continues, "Sufi tradition has a long history in Bangladesh, and the Pīrs constituted the main avenue by which Bengalis were introduced to Islam" and "shrines to revered saints" and the rooms where living Pīrs receive pilgrims "brim with activities and are part of the fabric of Bengali society in Bangladesh."⁴ General Ershad, the former military ruler (1982–1990), was a devout disciple of Pīr Atroshi (or Athrassi) and spared no "expense to spend time" with him.⁵ He addressed him as "*amar huzur*" (my Lord) "like any ordinary *murid*" (disciple).⁶ Pīrs are venerated throughout Bangladesh including some who were actually Hindus and Buddhists. Animals and natural objects were also purified, a term coined by Asim Roy (1982) in his pioneering study of how Ṣūfīs became cultural mediators between exogenous Islam and Bengal's endogenous religious traditions.⁷ Ṣūfī teachers played a major part in extending

   2. Uddin, *Constructing Bangladesh*, 146.
   3. Lewis, *When Cultures Collide*, 447.
   4. Uddin, *Constructing Bangladesh*, 146.
   5. Uddin, *Constructing Bangladesh*, 139.
   6. Dey, *Ṣūfism in India*, 28.
   7. Roy, *Islamic Syncretistic Tradition in Bengal*, 209.

agricultural space by clearing forest across the delta. Eaton (1993) describes this as a process by which Islam was spread not as some think by the sword but rather by the "ax and plow"[8] Esposito, Voll, and Bakar (2008) refer to sixty-two Pīrs, "mythical and historical" whose shrines are visited by "hundreds of thousands of pilgrims every year."[9] They also describe the emergence in "recent years" of urban-based Ṣūfī Pīrs, who enjoy a "large following among military officers, government officials, college and university teachers, and businessmen and politicians."[10] Quite a "large number" of Bangladeshis, they say, "identify . . . with some Pīr, living or dead" to whom they look for "spiritual guidance" and even for "intercession for the solution of their worldly problems."[11] One Pakistani Pīr visits Chittagong annually and collects a large amount of money from that city's "rich business community."[12] I often saw devotees collecting funds for their shrine by the roadside, stopping traffic to do so. Pīrs channel the divine, having achieved union with God. Before flying to Bangladesh, I did not know much about Ṣūfism, although I knew that it was Ṣūfī missionaries who had evangelized Bengal and that much Bangladeshi Islam has a Ṣūfī flavor. My experience of Islam in Bangladesh as well as among Bangladeshis in diaspora alerted me to the importance of Pīrs for many Muslims in their personal quest for fellowship with God. This stimulated further study. At some point, I also turned to consider the role of saints in the Christian tradition. Belonging to a denomination that does not celebrate the feast days of saints or possess any official teaching about saints, this was an informative venture. My encounter with Islam has often led me to learn more about aspects of my own religion. I began by asking what was it about Pīrs or Ṣūfī saints that attract Muslims, helping to nourish their religious experience and assisting them along the spiritual journey. Then I asked whether similarities exist between their role and that of Christian saints. Finally, I asked, if so, can this contribute in any way whatsoever to Christian-Muslim discourse on Jesus' as God made flesh? During two visits to Bangladesh while researching my 1998 book, *In Search of Muḥammad*, I asked interviewees questions about the role of Pīrs as I had asked Bangladeshis in Birmingham years before. I refer to this fieldwork below.

8. Eaton, *Rise of Islam*, 309.
9. Esposito et al., *Asian Islam*, 60.
10. Esposito et al., *Asian Islam*, 60.
11. Esposito et al., *Asian Islam*, 60.
12. Esposito et al., *Asian Islam*, 60.

IN SEARCH OF UNDERSTANDING

Saints in Islam

What follows does not attempt to describe every aspect of Saints in Islam or of their role in Ṣūfī tradition, which is outside the specific scope of this chapter. Rather, I focus on how their followers understand their relationship with God, whom some say "dwells in them." If God does dwell within them, this invites a conversation with what Christians mean by "incarnation." Ḥulūl has often been compared with incarnation; Nicholson (1914) cites Abu Nasr al-Sarraj (d. 998), "Some mystics . . . have erred in their doctrine that when they pass away . . . they enter into the qualities of God," continuing, "this leads to incarnation (*hulul*) or to the Christian belief concerning Jesus."[13] I bought my copy of Nicholson's introduction to Ṣūfism soon after arriving at Selly Oak. This was one of the first books about Islam that I obtained. Although I routinely cite some passages in my teaching as examples of Orientalist bias, *The Mystics of Islam* is still a useful primer. On Orientalist texts I tell students that once we are aware of bias we should not throw the proverbial baby out with the bath water. Ibn Taymīyya (1263–1328), mentioned in chapter 1 discussing his response to Paul of Antioch, dismissed "indwelling" with reference to Pīrs, the Shī'a imams, and Jesus. The term, he said, was unscriptural. Ṣūfīs were worse than Christians for claiming union with God, since at least the latter make the claim on behalf of a true prophet.[14] Christians, though, have seized on possible common ground here as a discussion platform, which may explain why an *Encyclopedia of Christianity* (1991) has an excellent article on "Sufism" by Ahmet T. Karamustafa. After describing the term used for Muslim saints, I turn to discuss the idea of *ḥulūl*, or divine indwelling, a controversial topic in Islamic discourse. The term for "saint," *walī* (trusted one, or friend), is derived from a Qur'anic passage such as 10:62, "Behold, verily, on the friends of Allah there is no fear, nor shall they grieve." The plural is ʾ*awliyāʾ*; women can be *walī* too and include the famous saint Rābiʿa (d. 801 CE), a pioneer of "love" mysticism in Islam. *Walī* is usually rendered "saint" in English. Several terms, including Pīr, Sheikh, and Marabout, depending on geographical location (respectively Persianate world, Arabic world, and Africa), signify the teacher or guide, the *Murshid*, who enjoys the status of a *walī*. Traditionally, saints trace a spiritual lineage or initiatic chain back to Muḥammad (the *silsilah*). In other words, the living

---

13. Nicholson, *Mystics of Islam*, 157.
14. Michel, *Muslim Theologian's Response*, 343–44.

Pīr is appointed by a predecessor, who himself succeeded his own teacher, stretching back to Muḥammad as the first teacher. One who follows a Pīr is a *murid*, or student, and more often than not offers an oath of loyalty. Many Pīrs, although not all, are heads of an organized order, a Ṣūfī *tarīqah*. A *tarīqah* is a path and all Ṣūfīs are *salik* (plural *salikun*, journeyers) as they travel from self-centeredness toward God-centeredness, from a false self-awareness (the *nafs*) toward *fanā*, the passing away of "self" into God-consciousness, also described as *baqā'*. This is often translated as "union with God." It can be understood as the realization that only God exists, that you "subsist" within God. It is from this that the concept of *ḥulūl*, or "divine indwelling," evolved. What really matters for the *murids* is that the *murshid* has completed the journey, so can channel the divine into their lives, or point the way toward the journey's end. As a friend of God, the Pīr is a conduit of divine grace (*karāmāt*) and divine blessing (*barakah*). The latter may manifest as miracles granted the Pīr by God. *Karāmāt* may be rendered as miracle, or act of grace.

Ḥulūl has always attracted controversy and censure, so much so that Ṣūfīs themselves have either avoided using the term or offer various defenses of those who felt compelled to express this. Commonly, defenses suggest that when Ṣūfīs use the language of union or imply that they enjoy this state, they misspeak or mistakenly speak about the unspeakable. What Ṣūfīs really experience, said al-Sarraj, is the surrender of their will to God so that God's will and their own will coincide in absolute harmony:

> When a man goes forth from his own qualities and enters into the qualities of God, he goes forth from his own will and enters into the will of God, knowing that his will is given to him by God and that by virtue of this gift he is severed from regarding himself, so that he becomes entirely devoted to God; and this is one of the stages of Unitarians.[15]

It was al-Ḥallāj who expressed *ḥulūl*, crying out "*ana al-Haq*" (I am Truth), which his opponents took to be a claim of divinity since "truth" is an attribute of God. Found guilty of heresy, he was crucified in 922 CE. Nicholson commented, "The doctrine of personal deification, in the peculiar form which was impressed upon it by Ḥallāj, is obviously akin to the central doctrine of Christianity, and therefore from the Moslem standpoint, a heresy."[16]

---

15. Nicholson, *Mystics of Islam*, 95.
16. Nicholson, *Mystics of Islam*, 90.

What al-Ḥallāj experienced was intimacy with God, the passing away of the "illusion of subject and object" so that he felt that he had "broken through to the Oneness" and could "either deny that he is anything or affirm that he is all things."[17] He wrote:

> I am He whom I love, and He whom I love is I:
> We are two spirits dwelling in one body.
> If thou seest me, thou seest Him,
> And if thou seest Him, thou seest us both.[18]

Knysh writes that sainthood was "particularly suspicious in the eyes of the guardians of Islam's purity" because if Ṣūfīs claim that saints, like Muḥammad, "have direct access to the source of divine revelation"[19] they usurp Muḥammad's role. Ibn ʿArabī refers to the fact that *walī* is applied to both God and man, whereas the word "prophet" is attributed exclusively to man.[20]

Explaining why al-Ḥallāj was not really a heretic but still wrong for expressing his inner experience of intimacy with God as he did, al-Ghazālī said that he misspoke. In the ecstasy and intoxication (*Wajad*) of *baqāʾ*, "drowned in the absolute of Oneness," he and others become "lost in" the "Abyss . . . they become persons struck dumb, and they [have] no power within them except to recall God" not "even the power to recall themselves." Thus "there remains with them nothing but God." "Drunk with a drunkenness wherein the sense of their own intelligence" disappears, they cry out words that should remain hidden "and not spoken."[21] Rūmī (1207–1273) explained "mystical *ḥulūl*" by saying that his sense of self receded, leaving only awareness of God:

> There's nothing left of me. I'm like a ruby held up to the sunrise.
> Is it still a stone? Or a world made of redness? It has no resistance to the sunlight.[22]

The saint's will, desire, and self becomes so completely aligned with God that they "flow into God." Notice how here the movement reverses the flow

---

17. Nicholson, *Mystics of Islam*, 97.
18. Nicholson, *Mystics of Islam*, 90.
19. Knysh, *Ibn ʿArabi*, 53.
20. Knysh, *Ibn ʿArabi*, 321n97.
21. Peters, *Reader on Classical Islam*, 342–43.
22. Berjak, "Suffism," 277.

that Christians traditionally associate with Jesus, who was God made man, not a man who flowed "into God." Karamustafa writes:

> The Sufi . . . could flow into God, but movement in the other direction was off limits, or at least extremely limited, since such as flow from the divine into the human could pave the way for divinization of the human and thus led to the suspect, even heretical, doctrine of incarnation and inherence (*hulul*).[23]

Does this undermine the possibility of identifying common ground between *ḥulūl*, saints, and Jesus' as God incarnate? Not necessarily, if we pause for a moment to consider "why" Islam is reluctant to speak of movement from the divine to the human. Jones lists several Muslim objections to incarnation, including "to attribute a son to the Divine Being in a literal sense is to attribute an imperfection to him which is met with in human beings," "has Allah a wife that he should have a son," and "communion is not attained by bringing down God to man in the sense of incarnation, but by man rising gradually."[24] The last objection informs the idea that flow is from the human to the divine not vice versa. Jones suggests that the rather crude ideas of sexual relations between God and a consort refer to stories associated with pre-Islamic Arabian deities.[25] However, when Global Partners translated the Gospel of Mark into Musulman Bangla in 2005 they courted controversy by choosing *Massih* (Messiah) for Son of God, and "Lord of all the Worlds" for Father. The traditional terms, they said, automatically imply that Jesus' birth involved sexual intercourse between God and a partner, causing Muslims unnecessary offence. *Massih* though, was later amended to "God's Uniquely-Intimate Beloved One." Other Bible translations into Muslim idiom have followed this convention. While this choice of Islam-sensitive language has been criticized, as a preacher I try to use gender-neutral language because I am convinced that God has feminine and masculine attributes and that, as God incarnate, Jesus was also in substance female and male although what people saw when they encountered him was his accidental, male appearance. This resembles how, in Catholic thought, the consecrated bread and wine maintain their accidental appearance but are transubstantiated into Jesus' body and blood. I prefer Creator, Redeemer, and Sustainer over Father, Son, and Spirit.

23. Karamustafa, "Ṣūfism," 222.
24. Jones, *Christianity Explained*, 57.
25. Jones, *Christianity Explained*, 57.

Is there any plausible reason why we should place limits on what God can and cannot do?

Jones says that in "seeking to safeguard the High and Lofty One from what he deems derogatory" the Muslim "is persuading himself that he knows the Mind of the Eternal." We do indeed possess knowledge of God but we cannot "speak as though the view-point of the Deity were our own."[26] The Qur'ān affirms God's absolute, not limited, power. A God who can say "be" and "it is" (Q3:47, 59) so that Mary conceives Jesus without sexual congress is also able to pass into the human realm, which, as God's own creation can in some respects be understood as an extension of God God's-self? I argue that God created us to enjoy direct communion with God but that sin and forgetfulness on our part prevents this, separating us from God. God moves toward us in love and mercy to save us from ourselves and to unite us with God's-self. What lies at the root of the concept of sainthood in Islam is the belief that the saint's will and God's will correspond exactly. Whether they pass into God or God passes into them may be playing with words, a matter of semantics. What people intend to explain is their experience of intimacy with God, an experience that no human vocabulary can adequately describe. Perhaps talk of movement of one to the other is itself metaphorical, since what really happens is the dissolution of any barrier between us and God and vice versa.

Before turning to Christian saints, a word about the other Muslim criticism of the *walī*, that they usurp Muḥammad's role. There is a story about Muḥammad appearing in a dream to Rābiʿa to challenge her if she truly loved him, presumably because she did not constantly refer to him in her discourse. She replied, "O prophet of God, who is there who does not love thee? But my love to God has so possessed me that no place remains for loving or hating any save Him."[27] Rābiʿa rightfully pointed out that, once the *salik* has traveled to the end of the journey, there is room for none but God yet it seems to me that without Muḥammad's example, there would be no *walī*. Rābiʿa had to follow Muḥammad to reach the goal. Once there, Muḥammad recedes, since his task is complete. The path that Ṣūfīs walk, the religious ideas they employ, all stand on Muslim ground. They imitate Muḥammad, not anyone else. When they proclaim the *shahadah* (*šahādah*), they declare that Muḥammad is the messenger of God. In interviewing Bangladeshi villagers, I asked them whether the role of Pīrs

---

26. Jones, *Christianity Explained*, 69.
27. Smith, *Muslim Women Mystics*, 123–24.

relegates "Muḥammad to a less significant role?" In reply, they suggested genuine Pīrs, not moneymaking charlatans, do not usurp Muḥammad's place because they "point to the Pīr, who is Muḥammad."[28] The existence of saints in Islam can be taken as proof that the path Muḥammad taught and walked leads people into a loving, intimate relationship with God.

Christian Saints

Christian saints are those whose lives exhibit high levels of holiness, whose words and acts mirror Jesus'. In Colossians, all Christians are referred to as "saints"(*hagiooi*) (Col 1:2). Later, the designation was restricted to a smaller number of Christians whose lives stood out, even among other Christians, as especially holy. In early Christianity, there was no formal procedure to determine sainthood. Later, a complex canonization mechanism was created. One criterion was sound doctrine, another proof that miracles were associated with the saint. Saints are also those in whose lives the Holy Spirit operates, which all Christians believe to be true of their experience. Just as Muslim saints follow the path of Muḥammad, so Christians follow Christ's. The Muslim saints' experience of intimacy with God, of *taqwā* stands on Muḥammad's prior experience, while the experience of intimacy with God of Christian saints stands on that of Jesus. For Christians, says Jones, "the voice of conscience itself is proof to us that the Divine Spirit can and does indwell man, while the lives of prophets and saints bear witness to the way in which God's Spirit endues man with power and insight."[29] God created people in a way that makes it possible for them to "receive such Divine self-impartation," the "quality and intensity" of which "depends ... upon the receptiveness of the individual."[30] In Jesus, the movement of the Divine toward the human met with "a perfect human response." Thus, God could reveal through Jesus God's redemptive purpose. Christians, of course, regard Jesus as unique among men but nonetheless as a man. Jones says that it was Jesus' consciousness of his intimacy with God as Father that led to his followers recognizing that as well as being a man Jesus was also God's son in a very special way. He points out, though, that when Christians began to speak of Jesus as God's son and as the Second Person of the Trinity, most of them were Jews for whom the conviction that there is only One God

28. Bennett, *In Search of Muhammad*, 199.
29. Jones, *Christianity Explained*, 71.
30. Jones, *Christianity Explained*, 71.

was unshakable. They chose the language they used "due to the poverty of human language" as an attempt to describe their "apprehension of the redemptive operation of God's Holy Spirit within us" but they did not for a moment intend to compromise their monotheistic faith.[31] Jesus was so intimately linked to their experience of God and of God's Spirit that they felt compelled to express this through language that spoke of a triune God despite this offending Jews who had not embraced Christianity. They "concluded that Christ belonged, is some mysterious way, to the category of 'God.'"[32] However, "no Christian claims that even the most widely accepted definition of the Trinity is adequate to the ultimate truth about God."[33] Hick refers to this attempt to explain Jesus' relationship with God as poetic. In his view, what began as "metaphorical poetry" morphed into "metaphysical" prose and ought to be revisited and re-expressed using modern idiom.[34]

Muslims have never called Muḥammad "God" or applied to him the language of divine sonship, although it can be argued that some Muslims approach the former, as Kenneth Cragg comments:

> Islam, in spite of itself, finds place for categories of relationship between divine ends and human means, between the eternal and the historical, unlike and yet akin to those that are at the heart of Christian experiences in Jesus as the Christ.[35]

Yet just as Christians believe that Jesus leads them to communion with God, so Muslims believe that Muḥammad's role of pointing the way toward God is essential. In Islam, it is Muḥammad's experience of intimacy with God that pioneers the way for those who replicate this in their own lives, becoming *walī*. For Christians, Jesus is the "pioneer and finisher of our faith" (Heb 12:12), who shows us the way. Arguably, Muslims and Christians use different language to describe the same experience, the same mystery. Given that the experience behind the language is a mystery, all language used in description is allegory and metaphor, not scientific. I agree with Hick on this. Both descriptions may be true yet neither may represent the whole of the truth. Jesus, for Christians, was "God" as well as a man yet exactly how Jesus was God and at the same time "man" has proved extremely difficult

---

31. Jones, *Christianity Explained*, 93–94.
32. Jones, *Christianity Explained*, 91.
33. Jones, *Christianity Explained*, 94.
34. Hick, *Universe of Faiths*, xi.
35. Cragg, *Muhammad and the Christian*, 65.

to define. Traditionally, Christians affirm that God's eternal Word entered a human embryo, that of Jesus. Jesus was then born as a man, with a human mother, Mary but without a human father. Most Muslims also accept the Virgin Birth of Jesus, based on such passages as Q3:47 and 3:59. Q3:52 compares Jesus with Adam because neither had a human father. Jesus was "created by a miracle."[36] I return to the issue of how Jesus was both wholly God and wholly man in my next chapter.

Toward Rapprochement

For their part, Muslims argue that God's eternal word was revealed through Muḥammad as a Book. Both the man Jesus and the Book revealed through Muḥammad represent finite physical objects. Yet God's eternal word dwelt or dwells within these physical objects. This does not imply that the whole of God resided or resides therein but that a quality or aspect did. Muslims use the term *Ṣifāh* (attribute). Traditional Christian language uses "person," which Muslims find objectionable, although it also used "hypostasis" (essence). This quality or person, though, is wholly divine. What Christians see in Jesus is the movement of God toward humanity, to save and to redeem, so that Jesus' life, death, and resurrection represent definitive moments in the history of the divine-human encounter. What we affirm when we say that God or God's word dwelt in Jesus is that God was present in him in a unique and special way. I can affirm that Jesus was God or God made flesh without knowing how. As I have written:

> I do not know whether Jesus was ontologically God, or whether he was so intimate with God that the distinction between who he was and who God is became blurred, which Muslims describe as a harmony of Jesus' will with God's will.[37]

In that statement, I had in mind Friedrich Schleiermacher's "god-consciousness" concept, which intrigued me at Manchester. In Schleiermacher's thought, Jesus' complete "god-consciousness" blurred, in him, the divine-human distinction, which makes it possible for Christians to regard him metaphorically as Son of God without belief in a supernatural birth or, as Hick argues, in his sharing God's "substance."[38] Hick's mythological

---

36. See Jones, *Christianity Explained*, 158.
37. Bennett, *Christian-Muslim Relations*, 215.
38. Hick, *Universe of Faiths*, 151.

explanation of incarnation argues that seeing the divine-human relationship in Jesus in terms of the "continuity" of divine love "may be more intelligible today" than talking about "the oneness of substance." Both formulations, according to Hick, "express the same faith" in different ways.[39] Hick's rethinking of salvation and Jesus' status began after he became a professor at Birmingham in 1967 as a result of his exposure to the Buddhist, Hindu, Muslim, and Sikh communities in the city.[40] He describes his option as "seeing Jesus as a human being rather than as the Second Person of the Trinity living as a human being,"[41] which *prima facie* resembles how Muslims understand Jesus. However, the crucifixion (which Hick does not reject) remains at issue. This is the subject of chapter 4 of this book. Hick called for a shift from a christocentric to a God-centered theology. His writing on pluralism did much to stimulate theological reflection on the challenge he described as Christian theology's "inability to proceed . . . as though Christianity were the only religion in the world." "Surely," he wrote, "our thinking must be undertaken, in the 'one-world' of today and tomorrow, on a more open and global basis."[42] In fact, Hick wanted to see theologians from a range of religions working together on understanding "all genuine human experience of the divine transcendence" in what has been called an exercise in World Theology.[43] This would not be "sectional but global" in the "use of religious data."[44]

Personally, I do not feel the need to reject any supernatural aspect involved in the incarnation because I refuse to place constraints on God's ability to act as God wished in order to restore to health what had become unhealthy, that is, human life, that of other created beings, and the planet itself. I can affirm that somehow "God made God's word enter Muḥammad, and pass through him into what became a physical, material object, a book" while remaining unable to explain the mechanics involved. This echoes with an Islamic expression that invites us to affirm certain truths about God such as that God sees and hears "without asking how" (*billa kayfa*) thus avoiding the picturing of God anthropomorphically as possessing eyes and ears. "The actual process of *incarnation* and of *bookification*," I continue

39. Hick, *Universe of Faiths*, 164.
40. Hick, *Universe of Faiths*, x.
41. Hick, *Universe of Faiths*, x.
42. Hick, *Universe of Faiths*, x.
43. See Smith, *Towards a World Theology*.
44. Hick, *Universe of Faiths*, 103.

"can be regarded as mysteries while their reality and truthfulness can be affirmed." There is, of course, a difference here in that for Christians Jesus is God's word while Muḥammad, for Muslims, was the vehicle through which the word was revealed rather than the embodiment of the word. Muslims ascribe the divine quality to the Book, not to the Prophet and only ever speak of Muḥammad as a man. Yet, as described in chapter 1, they speak of him as a very special man, as unique, as the perfect man. Christians go further, applying God language to Jesus. While problematic for Muslims, this language may actually express the same conviction. In practice, the relationship between Muḥammad and the Qur'ān is so intimate, as noted in the previous chapter, that while theologically the correct parallel is Jesus with the Qur'ān not Jesus with Muḥammad, functionally Jesus and Muḥammad occupy "a commensurate place . . . in believers' hearts."[45] Muḥammad lived the message contained in the Book. He is the Book's best interpreter. Knowledge of his life sheds essential light on the Book's meaning. If we can speak of Book-Prophet as a single unit, there is a sense in which the "divine" also dwelt in Muḥammad. Muslims may object to this on the same grounds that they reject the idea that God dwelt in Jesus *if a literal meaning is intended*. My suggestion is that what we are describing is spiritual experience, so that all the language we use is metaphorical not literal, even poetic, to echo Hick.

If, as a Christian, I am able to accept that God spoke through Muḥammad and through Muḥammad's Book, does this mean that God speaks to me through the Prophet-Book revelation? This question is more fully explored in chapter 3. Some Christians, described in chapter 1, accept Muḥammad as a genuine prophet but argue that Muḥammad's message was intended for the non-Christian world. Personally, I do not have a problem accepting that God spoke through Muḥammad after speaking through Jesus, with the qualifier that God's word is always consistent. Anything that promotes hatred of others or the privileging of the few cannot, for example, be ascribed to God. The creeds that some Christians recite were written after the time of Jesus, as were the books of the New Testament. God continues to speak to us through saints, too. Following Jones, I can affirm that the self-revelation of God in Jesus "is in every way adequate to human need." I agree with Jones that it is "distinctive," that "there can be no uncertainty about the quality of the life revealed," yet I also agree with him that we "cannot claim

---

45. Bennett, *In Search of Muhammad*, 227.

that God" in "Jesus in exhaustively revealed."[46] We cannot limit God, claiming that his "word" exhausted itself in Jesus. God still speaks. I believe that God spoke through Muḥammad and through his Book. Jesus, for me, represents the defining paradigm of divine love in action. Muḥammad, for me, adds important detail to the demand to order the whole of society so that human action harmonizes with God's will, upholding justice, treating all people with equity, alleviating poverty and suffering, ending exploitation and the elevation of profit and power over quality of life. Some Ṣūfī orders have distinguished histories of humanitarian and philanthropic service and of ordering their communities so that economic justice is achieved. Ṣūfī saints usually live as married men and women, so show those of us with families and jobs in the world that we can achieve harmony with God in the midst of human society. Rābiʿa was celibate but this is the exception in Islam not the rule. Many Christian saints were celibate. They lived lives isolated from the world so teach us little about what we might call the external aspects of living in harmony with God's will. Like Jesus, they teach us more about the inner life of faith. The "officially recognized" saint that has most attracted my interest is Francis of Assisi, yet he wrote such a strict rule for his community that it was modified before the church would sanction it. As inspirational as his life is, which, of course, is also instructive for Christian-Muslim dialogue,[47] his example doesn't help us to put food on the table, to pursue a career in the work-a-day world of family, of marriage or to fulfill our responsibilities within the wider society toward the body politic, encouraging good governance and global responsibility.

    I argue that "if neither Muslims nor Christians insist on the absolute nature of their doctrinal articulations, movement towards God and away from either of our formulations takes place."[48] By insisting that the language we use to describe the most intimate, transforming aspects of the divine-human relationship exhausts everything that can be said or is completely comprehensive and adequate, we elevate doctrine above spiritual experience. Doctrines are essentially human effort to describe what transcends our finite natures. This experience cannot be fully comprehended or rendered into language. By elevating our doctrines above experience, we lift the human above the divine. While Muslims may choose to see this as *širk*, or the false attribution of a partner to God, I contend that the lives of saints

---

46. Jones, *Christianity Explained*, 75–76.
47. See Moses, *Saint and the Sultan*.
48. Bennett, *Christian-Muslim Relations*, 216.

who, following Jesus' path, shone with God's presence and goodness, indicate that we also can experience what they experienced. The lives of those who achieved sainthood in Islam by imitating Muḥammad's example show us that intimacy with God and selfless service are real, achievable goals. Of course, this depends on accepting that Ṣūfī saints can attain communion with God; some Christians argue that even as great a Ṣūfī as al-Ghazālī could only seek God, that without faith in Jesus he did not find God. For example, Samuel Zwemer described al-Ghazālī as a Muslim "seeker after God," adding that "no one can read the story of al-Ghazālī's life, so near and yet so far from the Kingdom of God, so eager to enter and yet always groping for the doorway, without fervently wishing that al-Ghazālī could have met a true ambassador of Christ."[49] Jones argued that what matters is not the Name but "the experience of His redemptive work in our hearts and lives"[50] so a Muslim can be saved without having named the name of Jesus. In chapter 4, I describe a recent book by Elizabeth Johnson in which she questions how Christians have tended to view Christ's work as saving for humans while neglecting that he also offers other species and the planet renewal and redemption, "over the centuries Western theology's focus on sin became so intense that the wideness of God's saving mercy throughout the whole created world was by and large overlooked. . . . It is hard," she continues, "to take cosmic redemption seriously if redemption is only about forgiveness of human sin."[51]

Conclusion

Does an examination of sainthood in Islam and Christianity, then, establish any common ground that can reduce the Christian-Muslim divide on Jesus as God-incarnate? I suggest an affirmative answer, provided that, when we speak of divine indwelling with reference to Jesus or to the Ṣūfī saints, we are affirming that what people experienced was profound intimacy with God, which even the language of "indwelling" and "incarnation" only provisionally describes. The hymn "None of Self and All of Thee" expresses, for me, the aim of Christians and of Muslims who set out to imitate the pioneer of their respective faiths and of and those who have replicated this experience:

49. Zwemer, *Moslem Seeker*, 21.
50. Jones, *Christianity Explained*, 80.
51. Johnson, *Creation and the Cross*, xxi.

Higher than the highest heaven,
Deeper than the deepest sea,
Lord, Thy love at last has conquered:
"*None* of self, and *all* of Thee."
None of self, and *all* of Thee,
None of self, and *all* of Thee,
Lord, Thy love at last has conquered:
"*None* of self, and *all* of Thee"[52]

The hymn is based on John 3:30. Jones suggested that if, when we use God-language of Jesus in dialogue with Muslims, we explain that this is an "attempt" to describe "our apprehension of the redemptive operation of God's Spirit in our lives within us," while this "might still seem unacceptable" to them they may also "see that it is no longer unreasonable and certainly not blasphemous."[53] If Christians insist on elevating Jesus over the revelation through the Prophet-Book event, or Muslims insist on claiming that the Book-Prophet event supersedes the Christ-event, Muslims and Christians will remain at odds. My challenge is to view both revelatory events as equally significant and important, complimentary and mutually enriching.

---

52. Arranged by Theodore Monod (public domain), available at http://library.timelesstruths.org/music/None_of_Self_and_All_of_Thee.

53. Jones, *Christianity Explained*, 93.

Chapter Three

Can Christians with Integrity Regard the Qur'ān as a Word from God?

Setting the Scene

GIVEN that the majority of Christians have had little appreciative to say about Muḥammad, it is not surprising that they have seen the Qur'ān as equally problematic. As I have already argued, the Muḥammad-Qur'ān relationship is so intimate that the messenger cannot be evaluated without also evaluating the message. Most Christians, of course, regard the Qur'ān as written by Muḥammad, or compiled by him from existing sources for his own malign purposes. Muir's description of it as a "storehouse of Mahomet's own word"[1] totally rejects Muslim belief that the Qur'ān's content is word-for-word divine speech, as revealed to Muḥammad, between 610 and 632 CE. Some Christians ascribe a satanic origin. After describing my own journey into a deeper appreciation of the Qur'ān, this chapter describes Muslim reverence for the Qur'ān to set the stage for discussing why Christians have had so much difficulty accepting it as God's word. As we will see, many Christians perceive that the Qur'ān rejects foundational Christian beliefs about Jesus and the Trinity, and challenges the Bible's reliability. Against this negativity, I will formulate a case that Christians, while retaining their integrity, can regard the Qur'ān as a divine communication that supplements God's revelation in Christ. Inevitably, just as Christian discussion of Muḥammad tends to compare him with Jesus, so Christians make comparisons between Qur'ān and Bible even though, for many Christians, the latter witnesses the revelation through Christ and is not itself a revelation (although some Christians call it one). In Christianity, the

---

1. Muir, *Life of Mahomet*, 1:xxvii.

Bible is widely seen as inspired rather than revealed. Christ himself is the revelation. In Islam, Muḥammad was inspired when he spoke words that were later recorded as his *sunnah*, while the Qur'ān was revealed to him verbatim. However, this distinction is blurred by the term "unrehearsed revelation" which is also applied to the *sunnah* (accounts of Muḥammad's words and acts). In practice, some Christians view the Bible in ways that resemble how Muslims see the Qur'ān, by more or less ascribing all content to God. Therefore, in what follows, reference will be made to the Qur'ān-Bible relationship. When I posted on Facebook that I was beginning to write this chapter, one friend stated that his view of the inerrancy and infallibility of the Bible precluded any recognition of the Qur'ān as divine revelation. Some had no problem affirming that God can speak through the Qur'ān since God speaks through whatever medium God wishes. However, others said that it is also possible for Satan to speak through the Qur'ān, citing what they consider to be verses that sanction violence, the oppression of women, and other morally dubious acts.

My Encounter with the Qur'ān

My encounter with the Qur'ān began in September 1978 when I started my studies at Selly Oak. Before then, I had not even read a single verse in an English translation (the status of translations will be discussed below). Consequently, my initial exposure to the Qur'ān was through the Arabic. A major component of the Selly Oak course was learning to read and recite Qur'ānic verses in their original tongue. This process was supported by a native Arabic speaker who assisted with pronunciation (he was Egyptian) although David Kerr was our principal instructor. We mainly learned the shorter chapters, which are excellent examples of the Qur'ān's basic message and of its literary style, which is rhymed prose. I have already described how Kerr's obvious respect for the words of the Qur'ān gave me food for thought. Having not read it before this experience, I was open to what I would learn and to how I would think about the Qur'ān. In *Interpreting the Qur'an* (2010), which I dedicated to Kerr's memory, I wrote that "his love for the unspeakable eloquence of the Qur'an communicated itself through the passages he chose to teach." "We sat," I continued, "in the Old Library" where CSIC was then based, "sometimes as snow fell outside," reciting rhythmic chapters such as Surah 103 "with heart-felt conviction even as David corrected our errors."² I am to this day grateful that my initial encounter with the Qur'ān was through Arabic. Had I first read an English rendering, my mind would almost certainly have formed a different impression. Even the best other language renderings tend to be "clumsy and sometimes almost incoherent," lacking the poetic quality of the original. Unfortunately, not everyone has the opportunity to study Arabic. Many Christian acquaintances tell me that they find the Qur'ān repetitive, disorganized, and dull. This is "a far cry from what Muslims believe to be a book of unrivalled literary merit, because its origin is divine."³ Even leaving aside content with which Christians have theological issues, this creates an unfavorable impression that handicaps any development of an appreciation of the book that Muslims regard as an inimitable linguistic miracle (Q2:23; 11:13; 17:88; 52:34).

Rana Kabbani wrote that a non-Muslim or a non-Arabic-speaking Muslim reading the Qur'ān in translation read a different text. "The screen of imperfect translation," she says, prevents them from apprehending "this linguistic triumph." For those who do not know Arabic, it remains, she asserts, "a silent text" and "attempts to analyze it cannot do anything."⁴ My introduction to the Qur'ān at Selly Oak was in many respects closer to how Muslims first encounter the book—not by reading it from first page through to the last page but by reading chapters non-sequentially as they are chosen for content that speaks to particular concerns or contexts. Revealed, according to Muslims to Muḥammad in stages, chapter by chapter or at times, parts of a chapter, the content does not present a continuous narrative which frequently wrong foots non-Muslim readers. Different genres of content—devotional, moral, legal, exhortatory, stories about previous prophets—may be mingled together in a chapter, although some do contain a complete narrative. Sarwar and Toropov suggest that many misunderstandings arise from the assumption that the Qur'ān is "equivalent to the Judeo-Christian Bible or to the Hindu Bhagavad-Gita" or to "other religious texts." On the contrary, they say, the Qur'ān "is set apart from these texts . . . and, in fact, from all literature found on earth."⁵ This conviction that the Qur'ān, is unique in part informs the view that it cannot per se be rendered into other languages, thus "translations" are really commentaries

2. Bennett, *Interpreting the Qur'an*, x.
3. Bennett, *Interpreting the Qur'an*, 2.
4. Kabbani, *Letter to Christendom*, 34.
5. Sarwar and Toropov, *Idiot's Guide*, xix.

or interpretations. In this view, since the Qur'ān self-describes, in several verses, as a revelation in Arabic (Q16:103; 19:97; 41:2–4; 43:1–3) it ceases to be revelation when translated. Muslims also hesitate to refer to the Qur'ān as a "text," which implies that it can be analyzed and even deconstructed in the way that humanly composed texts are subjected to analysis. God's eternal, uncreated word cannot be scrutinized for development in literary style, as other texts can be. While non-Muslims complain about what they see as needless repetition in the Qur'ān, Muslims see this as reminding forgetful hearers (see Q39:23 for the Qur'ān's, self-awareness of repeating content) or as addressing different audiences, ranging from pagan opponents of Muḥammad, to his followers, to Jews and Christians. Experiencing the Qur'ān, write Sarwar and Toporov, has been compared to navigating a wild river, which "swirls and twists and turns, then doubles back from where it came . . . and then, just when one thinks one knows where the river is going, it curves again in an entirely new direction."[6] Some think it best for non-Muslims to read the Qur'ān's content in reverse, beginning with the shorter chapters toward the end and moving backward to read the longer chapters. Traditionally, chapters were revealed at Mecca (610–622 CE) or at Medina (622–632). The latter tend to be lengthier. As ordered toward the end of Muḥammad's life, chapters run (with the exception of the opening chapter) from longest (ch. 2, 286 verses) to the shortest (ch. 114, 3 verses, although number 108 has fewer words). However, not all non-Arabic-speaking Muslims view translations as different texts. A Muslim friend, whose Leeds master's thesis I examined, says that when she reads an English rendering, in her view, she is still reading the Qur'ān. In my opinion, while any serious student of Islam should acquire some proficiency in Arabic, informed reading of a translation can result in genuinely accessing the intent and meaning of the original. On the other hand, without additional help in understanding the content, translations are often off-putting, tedious, and opaque. Esask, pointing out how, post 9/11, sales of copies of translations rocketed, doubted that most people ended up reading more than a few pages, because "the Qur'an is a difficult book for strangers . . . and for many Muslims, to negotiate."[7] While I do not regard myself, by any stretch of the imagination, to be an Arabic scholar, there is little doubt that my ability to recite passages and to consult the original has greatly aided my effort to gain a deeper appreciation of the Qur'ān. In

---

6. Sarwar and Toropov, *Idiot's Guide*, 63.
7. Esack, *Qur'an: A User's Guide*, 109.

Bangladesh, it played a vital role in my outreach to my Muslim neighbors. An aim of this chapter is therefore to advise Christians on how best to read the Qur'ān, which was also the goal of my 2010 text. It took until 2010 for me to decide that my personal journey into an understanding of the Qur'ān had progressed enough, since 1978, to allow me to share my ideas and interpretations with others. Along that path, I read widely both Muslim commentaries and Christian attempts to reevaluate the Qur'ān, rather than dismissing it as contradicting Christian belief, or even as a satanic tool to undermine Christian truth. These evaluations remain available, of course, and some Christians will continue to endorse them. What follows expresses my conviction that, by dismissing the Qur'ān, we might be ignoring God's voice. It can be seen as an important reminder that God summons us to end oppression, idolatry, injustice, "to build a world of peace and prosperity for all people."[8] Just as I hesitate to claim that Christians can see Muḥammad exactly as Muslims do, so I hesitate to say that the Qur'ān can mean for Christians exactly what it does for Muslims. However, I do contend that a reevaluation can reduce the distance between what Muslims and Christians say about the book.

How Muslims See the Qur'ān

Much if not all of what Muslims believe about the Qur'ān is derived from what the Qur'ān says about itself. For Muslims, it is a revelation in Arabic, although addressed to all people (21:107). It sees itself as reminding the world of what God has already revealed through previous prophets, naming twenty-five. A traditions refers to 124,000. Its message and its messenger, the prophet Muḥammad, stand in continuity with Abraham and with all the biblical prophets, including Jesus, who was his immediate prophetic predecessor (2:163). The Qur'ān affirms the divine origin of earlier Books that were communicated to some of these prophets, naming the Torah, the Psalms, and the Gospel (the '*Injīl*, note use of the singular). It says that it confirms and corrects these (3:3), which Muslims see as a reference to their unreliability due to errors that have accidentally or deliberately corrupted these texts. In contrast, the Qur'ān is the book in which there is "no doubt" (2:2). God protects it from becoming corrupt (15:9). It is the criterion between right and wrong (3:4). Muslims view the Qur'ān as God's eternal, uncreated Word sent down via the angel Gabriel to Muḥammad

---

8. Bennett, *Interpreting the Qur'an*, x.

in stages (17:106) because if its content had descended at once (59:21) its potency would have shattered a mountain, let alone the Prophet's fragile body. The night on which Muḥammad received the first revelation, 96:1–4, is known as the Night of Power. This revelatory experience occurred while Muḥammad was meditating in a cave on a hill outside Mecca. Christians often say that he was in a trance, asleep, or in some way unconscious when the "revelation" came. This opened up all sorts of negative explanations, such as that this event was some type of psychotic episode, or resulted from an epileptic seizure. Many also claim that he fabricated or faked receiving revelation. Muḥammad himself describes perspiring heavily even on the coldest of days when revelation came and feeling his chest constricted so that words were forced from him. He also said that he was unaware of their meaning before the words left his mouth. He knew that a fresh revelation was coming when he heard the words, "In the Name of God, the Merciful Lord of Mercy" (the *basmala*). This formula opens every chapter except number 9. References in the Qur'ān to the "mother of the Book" (43:1–4) and to a "preserved Tablet" (85:22) inform the belief that before the content was sent down to Muḥammad it was transcribed onto a heavenly Tablet. How this happened and how content was communicated to Gabriel remains a matter of speculation. Muslims claim that the Qur'ān ends revelation, since the office of prophet culminated in Muḥammad, who was the "seal of prophecy" (33:40). This conflicts with the view of those Christians who regard prophecy as culminating with Jesus as Prophet, Priest, and King, although, as I stated in chapter 1, the office of prophet existed in the early church. Muslims stress Muḥammad's illiteracy (7:157) to emphasize that his role was passive in receiving the Qur'ān, to which he made no contribution. Stories of biblical prophets overlap considerably with biblical accounts. There is also additional material and some differences. Often, these stories are spread across chapters due to how the Qur'ān's content is organized. See Gabriel Said Reynolds (2018) for a comparative study with parallel texts from both scriptures. The Qur'ān shares fifty people with the Bible.

Al-Qur'ān (the Recitation) was always intended to be an aural and oral rather than a reading experience. Muḥammad and his followers memorized content. Shortly before he died, all 114 chapters were again recited by Gabriel, who checked the accuracy of Muḥammad's recall. It was then that each was given a name and their order fixed. Muslims usually refer to passages by their name. Citing passages by chapter and verse is a relatively recent Western convention complicated by the fact that versification can vary. Although not initially written down, scribes were eventually appointed who recorded passages using a variety of writing material such as pieces of bark, stones and parchment which were later collected and used to produce a complete written codex, a *mus'haf*. In 655 CE, under caliph ʿUthmān, a definitive version was commissioned, ratified by an expert committee. Although there have been developments in the Arabic script since then, Muslims believe that the content of their scripture remains unchanged. Quite recently, early portions of the Qur'ān have been discovered that tend to confirm this narrative. These fragments include two pages found in the Mingana collection at Birmingham in 2015, carbon dated to between 568 and 645 CE. Now catalogued as Mingana 1572a, I saw this parchment shortly after it came to light when it was placed on display at a reception hosted by Special Collections at the University's Cadbury Research Library to honor my friend and colleague David Thomas.

Physical copies of the Qur'ān are treated with respect. Muslims wash their hands before touching them. They are often kept on special stands. Muslims rarely place anything on top of a copy, or put it on the floor. As a first-year missionary in Bangladesh, I was rebuked for placing my Bible on the floor under a hymn book, suggesting that Bangladeshi Christians imitate their Muslim neighbors in how they treat their scripture. People who memorize the Qur'ān and master its recitation are greatly honored. Copies may be handwritten following one of the schools of calligraphy. Verses are inscribed on the walls of buildings, and on everyday objects, to remind Muslims of God's omnipresence. Passages are recited during each of the five daily prayers, repeating the opening chapter at the start of each unit or *rakʿah* before adding one of the shorter chapters.

The Qur'ān guides Muslim life. The Prophet is regarded as its best interpreter, which is why I have spoken of this intimate relationship in terms of the Book-Prophet event as being commensurate with the Christ-event in Christian thought. The *sunnah* is the main source for this as recorded in the classical *ḥadīth* collections. Directly, only four verses name the Prophet, but many others cannot be properly understood without knowing when content was revealed or, for Christian critics, invented in the context of his life. Here, the biographical works as well as the *ḥadīth* provide essential information. These give us the "situation of revelation" which are used in *fiqh*, jurisprudence, for determining whether a passage has universal applicability or was particular to the original context. Only the former could provide the basis of any legal construct. Similarly, only verses considered as clear (*Muhkam*, Q3:7) rather than allegorical (*Mutashabih*) could be used for legal purposes. Christians routinely seize on the term *Mutashabih*, often translated as unclear, to ridicule the Qur'ān for containing these opaque passages while also denying that other passages, such as descriptions of heaven and hell, and the story of Muḥammad's Night Journey and Ascent in the *sunnah* (briefly referred to at Q17:1) can be seen as allegory. Muslims, though, have been reluctant to put too much weight on the "situations of revelation" in case this implies that context somehow dictated content.[9] Esack's view of the Qur'ān, as an invitation to liberate the oppressed and build just, equitable societies, proposes that interpretation should always be grounded in context, calling for a link between exegesis and action. He rejects the contention that a single, fixed meaning can be retrieved from the Qur'ān, valid in all circumstances. He advocates a cycle of reflection, action, reflection, action in what is an ongoing process of shifting from text to context, "there is no end to God's promise to disclose."[10] "Liberation theology," he writes, "is the process of praxis for comprehensive justice, the theological reflection that emerges from it and the reshaping of praxis based on that reflection."[11] He has been criticized by some for opening up the hermeneutical task to all Muslims rather than defending the role of scholars as interpretive gatekeepers. In his native South Africa, Esack, later Commissioner for Gender Equality in Nelson Mandela's administration, was an anti-apartheid activist before the apartheid system collapsed. Esack convened base communities through his organization, Call of Islam, to study the Qur'ān through a liberational lens. He rejects the "wide acceptance, among the more conservative Muslims" that Q23:85 excludes Jews and Christians from salvation.[12] He argues that Muḥammad's call was sometimes to invite people to become Muslims, sometimes to "challenge them regarding their commitment to their own scripture (Q5:68), their deviation from these, and their distortion thereof."[13] Thus, religious diversity "is the will of God." Muslims who deny this and claim exclusive status for Islam are guilty of the exclusivism that the Qur'ān condemns in others

---

9. Esack, *Qur'an, Liberation & Pluralism*, 102.
10. Esack, *Qur'an, Liberation & Pluralism*, 111.
11. Esack, *Qur'an, Liberation & Pluralism*, 8.
12. Esack, *Qur'an, Liberation & Pluralism*, 164.
13. Esack, *Qur'an, Liberation & Pluralism*, 173.

(see Q2:111).[14] After Birmingham, Esack went to Frankfurt, Germany, for postdoctoral study in biblical hermeneutics.

Muslims debated many matters related to the Qur'ān, such as how to understand verses describing God as hearing, seeing, and siting on a throne and the relationship between God and God's attributes (*Ṣifāh Allah*) which, if coequal and coeternal with each other and with God, could compromise divine unity. This was especially true of the concept of the eternal word transcribed onto a Tablet. Some accused other Muslims of worshipping two Gods, and argued in favor of a Qur'ān that was created in time. Most ended up affirming belief in the uncreated and eternal Qur'ān. To a degree, this was influenced by Muslim awareness of Christian debate about whether Christ was eternally coexistent with God, or created in time and used similar terminology. Despite this, Muslims found Christian notions of Trinity and incarnation absurd. Muḥammad's acts and deeds that related to his mission are believed to have been inspired. However, forty *qudsi ḥadīth* are categorized as revelation although, unlike the Qur'an, their phrasing was formulated by the Prophet rather than communicated to him verbatim by God. Nonetheless, this represents authentic revelation that is outside the content of the Qur'ān. On the other hand, while Islamic thought has consistently regarded the whole of the Qur'ān as unquestionably revealed directly from God, the authenticity of *ḥadīth* has been and remains open to debate. Scholars categorize *ḥadīth* ranging from sound to weak. However, even *ḥadīth* classically placed in the highest category have been and are critiqued.

Why Have Christians Had So Much Difficulty Accepting the Qur'ān as God's Word?

Christian negativity toward the Qur'ān follows from the perception that to affirm a divine origin runs the risk of downgrading Jesus and the Bible. It would apparently deny that Jesus is God's son, the Trinity, and Jesus' death on the cross. If the Qur'ān is God's final revelation, Jesus must, Christians presume, be seen as an earlier, superseded revelation or as of secondary importance. This would resemble how Christians view the Hebrew Bible. It remains a valid source of instruction but the New Testament takes priority over it and much content is seen as redundant. Of course, Marcion (d. 160 CE), whose movement vied with the Roman church for domination and

---

14. Esack, *Qur'an, Liberation & Pluralism*, 159.

nearly won, rejected the whole Hebrew scripture. Most Christians see the sacrificial system, many commandments, and all the material about the temple as no longer valid. Effectively, Christians mine the Hebrew Bible for content that they believe predicts or anticipates Jesus, which they often interpret differently from Jews. It is more or less treated as a source of proof texts to support Christian convictions about Jesus. I sometimes say to my students that in sharing the Hebrew Bible Christians and Jews are divided by a common scripture. Recognition of acceptable content in the Qur'ān mingled with falsehood could resolve some of the problems associated with how Christians might view the Qur'ān, but requires criteria for determining what does and does not qualify. It would also undermine any possibility of affirming what Muslims believe about its divine origin. God would not reveal a scripture containing error. Error for Christians includes content they regard as contradicting other content. They have taken delight in ridiculing the interpretive device known as "abrogation," by which some passages cancel and replace others even though they regard the New Testament as superseding much of the Hebrew Bible. Christians have deconstructed the content of the Qur'ān tracing this to earlier sources, including non-canonical gospels, in a way that tends to see problematic content as originating with Muḥammad and material they find acceptable as copied from sources they deem genuine. Cragg, who spent a long life wrestling with how to reconcile what he saw as God's presence in Islam with his Christian convictions, insisted that the production of the Qur'ān must resemble that of the Bible, in which divinely inspired content and that created by fallible humans coexists. Again, Aydin critiques this as a Christianization of Islam: "He has tried to establish a truer and more complete interpretation of revelation by using Christian terms and categories."[15] The contention that, while God's voice may be heard speaking through the Qur'ān, some content is not of divine origin undermines Muslim conviction that their scripture is verbatim from God just as the Muslim denial of Christ's incarnation undermines this foundational Christian belief. Many Christians believe that biblical authors filtered inspired content through the lens of their personalities thus each of the four evangelists shaped their gospel accounts differently. From a Muslim perspective, Esack has raised questions about the boundary between revealed content and Muḥammad's consciousness, referring to the belief that revelation penetrated to his heart, where, he says, the divine encountered the human. He is open to the

---

15. Aydin, *Modern Western*, 156.

possibility that some content may contain the Prophet's thoughts as, conceivably, some material in the Qur'ān might properly belong to the category of the *qudsi ḥadīth* or vice versa. He refers to this as the "grey area" between Muḥammad's receipt of revelation and its publication.[16] Before completing his doctoral studies at Birmingham, Esack graduated from a traditional, conservative *madrasa* in Pakistan where he completed eight years of study. This takes Esack close to Cragg's position but leaves the question about how such content might be identified unresolved. Trained at Manchester in the form, source, and redaction critical approach to the Bible, which I find persuasive in many respects, I tend to ignore this when preaching. While criteria have been developed to support such judgments, these can also inject personal agendas into the process. We may determine that the early church inserted this or that content because we dislike it, while crediting Jesus with whatever fits our theology. Christians who deconstruct the Qur'ān have rejected what they call "higher criticism" when they turn to the Bible. For example, William St. Clair Tisdall wrote tracts against this approach to the biblical text but applied it to the Qur'ān. See his *The Original Sources of the Qur'an* (1905). In contrast, I have tried to deal with the whole of the biblical text as received today and, below, adopt the same approach vis-à-vis the Qur'ān.

The attempt to see whether Qur'ānic passages that represent a challenge for Christians can in any way be affirmed as vehicles for the divine word invites more reflection than simply declaring that these conveniently fail to qualify as genuinely from God. Chapter 4 discusses the specific issue of Jesus' crucifixion which merits a more detailed discussion because, for many Christians, it demolishes the very ground on which Christian thought stands. Below, I discuss the challenge presented by the Muslim claim that the Bible has been corrupted, and the charge that we exaggerate Jesus' importance again drawing on Lewis Bevan Jones. Some Christians, too, including a number who responded to my Facebook post about this chapter, take issue with the Qur'ān for other reasons, accusing it of justifying aggressive war, the oppression of women, and of non-Muslim minorities, resulting in the denial of many civil rights. These assertions cannot be adequately discussed in this current book. I explored most of these in my *Muslims and Modernity* (2005), where I analyzed a range of Muslim opinions on gender, human rights, and war and other contemporary issues.

16. Esack, *Qur'an: A User's Guide*, 113.

My voices included some that argue for compatibility between Islam and modern human rights, and that the Qur'ān supports this agenda.

A Proposal on How Christian Might, with Integrity, Regard the Qur'ān as God's Word

Accepting the whole of the Qur'ān as divinely revealed would seem to include recognition that, as transmitted to us today, the Bible is unreliable. In Islamic thought, this is referred to as *taḥrīf* (distortion, alteration). Based on Qur'ānic verses such as 2:77, 3:72, and 7:161–2 this has generated a great deal of Christian apology and anti-Muslim polemic. Often, the integrity of the biblical record is defended with reference to ancient manuscripts and citations by early theologians. Arguably, the form, source, and redaction critical approach accepts that there has been interpolation and revision of the biblical text. *Taḥrīf* infers that Jews and Christians deliberately tampered with the Bible's text to support their exaggerated claims, although application of this to the gospels may date from the work of Ibn Hazm (994–1064 CE), who has been credited as the first Muslim thinker to "systematize the doctrine of textual falsification."[17] My colleague in the CMR project Gordon Nickel adds that this became a standard theme in Muslim anti-Christian polemic.[18] Muslims have suggested that, since the Qur'ān refers to a single gospel not to the canonical four, the original scripture revealed to Jesus has been lost. This view also reflects Muslim awareness that the four gospels do not readily fit their concept of scripture as first person divine speech. Rather, it resembles, as Jones pointed out, *ḥadīth*, which, just as the gospel writers describe Jesus' deeds in their own words, contain not only Muḥammad's sayings but others' accounts of his acts.[19] Some Muslims see the *Gospel of Barnabas*, which Christian scholars deem a very late forgery, to be the real *'Injīl* because it mentions Muḥammad, is anti-Trinitarian and depicts Jesus being raised into heaven bypassing the crucifixion, all of which echoes Qur'ānic content. It reserves Paradise for men who are circumcised.

Jones points out that the Qur'ānic verses that Muslims cite on *taḥrīf* refer to Jews, not to Christians, and that the charge of altering appears to

---

17. Nickel, *Narratives of Tampering*, 23.
18. Nickel, *Narratives of Tampering*, 23.
19. Jones, *Christianity Explained*, 42.

be leveled at "some" or at "a party thereof"[20] not at all Jews. Referring to a publication by Sayyid Ahmad Khan (1817–1898), *Kitābu't Taḥrīf* (1862) Jones distinguishes between two types of textual alteration, namely of the text itself and of the text's meaning. Following Khan, Jones argues that these verses accuse some Jews of "making verbal changes when reading"[21] not of adding to or subtracting words from the text itself. Khan determined that the Qur'ān does not accuse either Jews or Christians with actually altering the biblical text. Khan had already turned to the task of writing a Muslim commentary on the Bible (between 1860 and 1865), an unheard-of venture for a Muslim thinker. Many Muslims have identified over a hundred contradictions in the Bible which they say undermines its credibility as scripture. For example they contrast Genesis 7:2 and 7:8–9 on how many animals entered Noah's ark, Exodus 15:3 on a God of war and 15:33 on a God of peace, Matthew 1:16 and Luke 3:23 on the name of Joseph's father, various verses on who saw Jesus' empty tomb, Genesis 1:25 and Genesis 2:18–19 on whether beasts or men were created first, and many other verses. Based on his doctoral work at Birmingham, Charles Ramsey analyzes Khan's pioneering commentary in his forthcoming *God's Word, Spoken and Otherwise: Sayyid Ahmad Khan (1817–1898)*. I had the honor of mentoring his master's dissertation at Baylor and of coediting our volume *South Asian Sufis* (2012).

Jones did not require Muslims to accept such doctrinal formulations as Trinity or incarnation as a condition for sharing the same experience of the divine that these tentatively and provisionally attempt to describe. My personal proposal is that, when reading a verse such as Q4:171, this can be interpreted as challenging a Christian theology that elevates belief in Trinity over the experience of inner renewal and the obligation to live lives characterized by love and generosity. The verse says, "The Messiah, Jesus, the son of Mary, was but a messenger of Allah and His word which He directed to Mary and a soul [created at a command] from Him. So believe in Allah and His messengers. And do not say, 'Three.'" In my view, Trinity is an acceptable way of describing our apprehension of the divine, but insistence on this expression can overlook the fact that ultimately God is beyond number. Therefore, overstressing Trinity obscures God's ultimate ineffability. Christians routinely deny belief in Three Gods and dismiss this verse as misinformed. Additionally, they suspect that Muḥammad thought that

20. Jones, *Christianity Explained*, 8.
21. Jones, *Christianity Explained*, 10.

the Trinity consists of God, Christ, and Mary (see Q5:116) and found this preposterous. Some Christians contend that Christians whom Muḥammad encountered held this false doctrine which he then rejected, thus his reference to "Three" explicitly condemned that regional heresy rather than a Triune theology as such. Yet are we still left with the charge of worshipping Three God's? My response here is to say that some Christians confuse the meaning of Trinity and actually do worship Jesus and the Spirit as distinct entities separate from the First Person of the Trinity. I believe that Christian worship should be of the First Person of the Trinity. We offer this through Jesus as directed by the Spirit but these should not be objects of our worship. Jesus did not invite anyone to worship him but, as the Qur'ān affirms (5:172), pointed to God as the sole object worthy of worship. Matthew 4:8 says, "You shall worship your God, and Him only shall thou serve," and John 4:11 says, "The hour is coming and now is, when" people "will worship the Father in spirit and in truth."

Conclusion

In conclusion, the question remains: even if recognizing the Qur'ān as communicating the divine word does not involve also accepting that the Bible has been corrupted, how do we reconcile Christian beliefs such as the Trinity and Jesus' divine and human natures with the Qur'ān's rejection of these? I have already referred to Jones's proposition, which is similar to Hick's more recent proposal, that the poverty of human language limited how Christians could express their threefold experience of the divine. Hick saw the "made flesh" language as poetic metaphor not as a statement of metaphysical fact. Arguably, neither the third-century articulations of the Trinity or of Jesus' divine and human natures are explicitly found in the New Testament. Tireless argument about whether Jesus had one nature or two and whether these were commingled or confused attempted what should have been left alone. My own view on Jesus as wholly divine and wholly human is that trying to understand Jesus' inner nature diminishes the mystery that lies at the heart of the incarnation of the eternal word as a flesh-and-blood human being in first-century Palestine. It is regrettable that pointless debates between monophysites, dyophysities, and others led to schism, as did the tedious debate about whether Jesus' substance was the same as (*Homoousios*) or similar to (*Homoiousios*) the Father's. Perhaps the Qur'an's challenge is to accept the mystery of incarnation as well as of the

Trinity without proposing any definitive articulation of their mechanics, which we cannot comprehend. In what it says about Trinity and incarnation, the Qur'ān can be seen as a post-biblical divine word reminding us that despite our best efforts God remains ineffable. Attempts to define these matters deflect us from what Muslims and Christian can agree, without resolving every paradox about Unity-Trinity or Jesus' humanity and divinity. Namely, that God invites us to reject idols, establish just societies and peace between nations, to respect the planet itself and all God's creatures as we worship the One God and live before that God lives of divinely gifted holiness in consciousness of God's omnipresence throughout the whole cosmos. I do not feel compelled to insist on the Christian view that the Qur'ān must contain material contributed by Muḥammad accepting that God's actions are not confined by the scope of our minds. Certain divine possibilities lie beyond human comprehension. Thank God for that, who, as Muslim scholars sign off their works, "knows best" (*Vallahu-alam*). Typically, Muslims say that when the Qur'ān differs from the Bible it is corrective of the latter while for some Christians the Bible always trumps the former. This insistence of one scripture taking priority rarely results in agreement. My tendency is to see both scriptures as offering a valid perspective, even if apparently contradictory, and to enquire how they might each deepen our understanding of God's purposes. Scriptural reasoning, which I describe in the final chapter, invites Jews, Christians, and Muslims to study each other's scriptures in small groups as a shared exercise of discovery, without compromising their deepest convictions, in a spirit of openness and mutual respect. I am convinced that Christians who become more familiar with the Qur'ān will, at the very least, find it harder to repeat traditional Christian criticisms of the book mentioned in this chapter.

Chapter Four

Is There Any Possibility of Rapprochement on the Issue of Whether Jesus Died on the Cross?

An Insistent Question

THIS was the question I discussed in my contribution to the first volume in the series on Christian reflections from Islamic contexts (2008). In that chapter, I described how my thinking had changed between writing *In Search of Muhammad* (1998) and *In Search of Jesus* (2001). Both books tried to create dialogue between my faith and the faith of Muslims, although the second text had a wider scope. It also explored Jewish, Hindu, Buddhist, and humanist images of Jesus. Kenneth Cragg contributed two chapters to the 2008 volume. His second chapter was more or less a response to mine, which the editor included in order to "return the cross to the centre of the historic Christian faith,"[1] since, in his view, I had de-centered it. Singh described my contribution as "controversial." I would characterize my chapter as a call to rethink the significance of the cross in response to the insistent challenge represented by the Muslim view. I was aware, when writing the chapter, that I would go too far for some. Recently, I have found an ally in the writing of Elizabeth A. Johnson, a feminist theologian at Fordham University and a Sister of St. Joseph of Brentwood. Beginning with the absence, or apparent absence, of the cross in Islam, this chapter compares my thinking in the two earlier books and concludes with observations drawing on Johnson's innovative scholarship. In reprising my 2008 chapter, I also introduce new material from subsequent reflection on the issue under review.

---

1. Singh, introduction to *Jesus and the Cross*, 4.

The Cross as a Scandal to Muslims

Christian thought regards the event of the cross—Jesus' death by crucifixion—as so central that it functions as the cornerstone or bedrock of Christian faith itself. Most Christians find the notion of Christianity without the cross unimaginable. How can they be cleansed by Jesus' blood if the crucifixion is fiction? On the cross, according to most Christians, one who had no sin, who did not deserve to die, died to take upon himself the sins of all humanity, making atonement and divine-human reconciliation possible. Jesus' death substituted for ours, since his death satisfied God by paying the price for our sins. St. Paul put it like this, "For as in Adam all die, so in Christ will all be made alive" (1 Cor 15:22). Not to preach Christ crucified denies the gospel. Paul preached "Christ crucified, unto the Jews a stumbling block, unto Greeks foolishness" (1 Cor 1:23). It is this intimate relationship between the traditional Christian doctrine of the atonement and the crucifixion (but see my concluding observations) that, as Ahmed Deedat (1918–2005)—the anti-Christian polemicist—put it in his hugely popular *Crucifixion or Cruci-fiction* (1984), produces the equation, "in a nutshell, No Crucifixion, No Christianity." Christian missionaries to Muslims have described the Muslim response to the crucifixion in similar terms; Samuel Marinus Zwemer (1867–1952) thought that what Islam needs most of all is the very cross which it not only rejects but sees as "foolish"; "if the Cross of Christ is the missing link in their creed, then the preaching of the Cross, although it may seem to them foolishness, will yet prove among Moslems the wisdom of God and the power of God."[2] Zwemer was well aware of the argument that, if the crucifixion did not happen, the Christian doctrine of the atonement—in traditional form—collapses. Thus, "the bitter attacks of Islam on Christianity in the Moslem press of Egypt and India nearly always find their centre in the Deity and the atoning work of Jesus."[3] Zwemer also pointed out that Muḥammad is said to have had "such a repugnance to the sign of the cross that he destroyed everything brought to his house with that figure upon it."[4] He cites the tradition that, when he returns to earth, Jesus will "break the crucifix." This alludes to the widespread Muslim belief that having been raised to the heavens by God to prevent the indignity of the cross (Q4:157), Jesus will return

---

2. Zwemer, *Moslem Christ*, 181.
3. Zwemer, *Moslem Christ*, 117.
4. Zwemer, *Moslem Christ*, 86–87.

before Judgment Day and play a role in the end time events. Zwemer wrote two books on the cross, *The Glory of the Cross* (1928) and *The Cross Above the Crescent* (1941). Cragg has described the redeeming death of Christ in terms of "cosmic significance." It is, he writes, a matter of profound concern that, in its rewriting the story of the cross, Islam "offends deeply against all that the gospels disclose about the self-giving of Jesus."[5] Islam, Cragg continues, says that this rewriting is "in the interest of God's glory," as "God cannot be honored in the victory of a prophet's foes."[6] I think, though, that there may be some scope here to ask whether the Qur'ān is so emphatic in rejecting that prophets can suffer. Muḥammad was ill-treated during his Meccan phase. His subsequent victories can be seen as divine vindication. At Q28:21, Moses had to flee from Egypt in fear of apprehension for murder. Q36:40 says that all prophets have been ridiculed. Muslims, however, typically see the slaying of a prophet as so insulting to God that God does not allow this to happen. In his first chapter in the 2008 volume, Cragg writes about the *hijra* as the parting of the way between an Islam that opted for power and a Christianity that chose sacrifice and suffering on behalf of others. Yet I would argue that Christians have not always eschewed power. Post Constantine, Christians have often embraced this as serving the ascended Christ who is King of kings, asserting the church as the highest civil authority even though it delegates the exercise of temporal power to others. Certainly, popes claimed for centuries to exercise three jurisdictions, the spiritual, the temporal, and over the realm of purgatory. Perhaps the *hijra* marks the ultimate triumph of the good over those who oppose this, as Jesus' resurrection defied his death.

Stressing the Why Not the What of Christian Belief

In my four decades of encounter with Muslims, what they perceive to be the scandal of the cross, represented by our most commonly used symbol, emerges as one of the most challenging and insistent issues. Other issues, such as the Trinity, Jesus' Divine Sonship, the character of Muḥammad, and the status of the Qur'ān, already discussed in this book, are also challenging; yet, following Lewis Bevan Jones, I am convinced that some sort of mutually acceptable understanding is possible when we admit the limitations of human language. I have found Jones's advice that, when we stress the

---

5. Cragg, *Call of the Minaret*, 271–72.
6. Cragg, *Call of the Minaret*, 268.

POSSIBILITY OF RAPPROCHEMENT ON WHETHER JESUS DIED ON THE CROSS

reason why we believe what we do about Jesus rather than the language we choose to express this, more common ground exists than we initially think. Trinity expresses our belief that we encounter God as creator, redeemer, and sustainer—but this can also be described by speaking of One God who reveals God's-self in a threefold way, or through three characteristics or modes of being—and does not have to describe these as Persons. This brings us closer to Muslim thinking about how the One God acts through multiple attributes which, while distinct and coequal, exist within God's oneness not as external to God or to each other.[7] Problems remain but some degree of rapprochement seems possible. The possibility of Christians viewing both the Prophet and the Qur'ān in ways that affirm that God speaks through both has been explored in this book which again reduces distance between Christians and Muslims. However, turning to the cross, this approach would appear to be stymied because we do not only have to deal with belief and interpretation but with the questions of historicity—either the cross happened, or it did not. If it did not happen, anything that Christians believe about its salvific significance rests on fiction. Cragg's position is that denying the cross is fake history. Here, the gospels are right and Muslims mistaken. He is insistent on the cross's historicity.[8] On the other hand, in his response to my 2008 chapter and elsewhere, Cragg argues that the cross is perhaps not so absent in Islam as we think. Here, he refers to Qur'ānic verses that speak of Jesus' death and resurrection (see 3:54; 19:33). Clearly, while Muslims see these as lying in the future while for Christians they have already happened, these verses are less problematic than a denial that Jesus' died on a cross over two thousand years ago. This denial rests on one of the most contested passages in Christian-Muslim relations, Q4:156:

> And [for] their saying, "Indeed, we have killed the Messiah, Jesus, the son of Mary, the messenger of Allah ." And they did not kill him, nor did they crucify him; but [another] was made to resemble him to them. And indeed, those who differ over it are in doubt about it. They have no knowledge of it except the following of assumption. And they did not kill him, for certain.

Cragg and others point out that the language and syntax here is complicated, which leaves room for different interpretations including the traditional Muslim view that Jesus was not crucified. However, it also permits some Muslims to suggest that Jesus was crucified but not killed on the cross.

7. See Bennett, "Christian Trinity and Muslim Attributes."
8. Cragg, *Call of the Minaret*, 267.

Later, after recovering in the tomb, God raised him up into the heavens. Perhaps the most widespread belief among Muslims, though, is that a substitute, probably Judas, was crucified instead of Jesus, whom God protected. Cragg writes, in his response to my 2008 chapter, that it is our Christology, which takes us "beyond" the historical, "for which the Qur'ān has neither place nor tolerance"[9] while arguing that, by including the above verse, the Qur'ān accepts that something happened on Good Friday. Christians have also read Docetic ideas into this passage which can be interpreted as saying that onlookers thought they witnessed Jesus' crucifixion but this was hallucinatory. The divine Jesus neither suffered nor died in the cross. William Temple Gairdner (1873–192) thought that the source of Muḥammad's information on Jesus was heretical gospels, which is itself a rebuke to Christians for failing to bear authentic witness.[10] Something of this is also found in Cragg's thought for whom Christian engagement with Islam is both a task of retrieval—searching for truth in Islam—and one of restitution—restoring what it fails to grasp. Yet Cragg does not think that the Qur'ān's denial of the crucifixion is as emphatic as either Muslims and Christians assume it is. The problem here, though, is that persuading Muslims that their traditional understanding of Q4:156 is wrong and that Jesus really was crucified still leaves the Christian idea of a sacrificial atonement obnoxious to them. I agree with Marshall (2001) that

> even if it could be established that the Quran does not teach that Jesus genuinely died on the cross and was then raised to heaven, this episode would still have to be interpreted within the Quranic frame of reference, which has no place for ideas of atonement . . . the events of Jesus' earthly life would not be seen as the key moment in God's redemptive plan.[11]

On the other hand, a few Muslims have contemplated how to see meaning in the cross without explicitly either rejecting or affirming its historicity. Cragg translated M. Kamel Hussein's *City of Wrong: A Friday in Jerusalem* into English, where he again referred to the ambiguity of Q4:156[12] and commended Hussein for writing about Good Friday in a way that transcended polemic and, "without transcending Quranic limits on which the Muslim belief that the crucifying of Jesus did not happen depends, makes

---

9. Cragg, "Qur'an and the Cross," 180.
10. Gairdner, *Rebuke of Islam*, 19.
11. Marshall, "Christianity in the Quran," 15.
12. Cragg, introduction to *City of Wrong*, 12.

a penetrating analysis of the will to His crucifixion."¹³ Hussein focuses on the crowd's intent to kill Jesus, who did not merit execution. Nowhere does the novel either affirm or deny the event of the cross but chooses to use what people intended to explore the human condition. Similarly, Hasan Askari uses Jesus' cry of dereliction from the cross as a segue to meditating on Muḥammad's sense of abandonment during the extended period of silence that followed receipt of the first revelation in 610, writing, "During this period, with all his trust in the Unseen, he must have gone through a profound sense of insecurity, and might have asked, deep within himself 'Why, why hast thou forsaken me?' . . . It is the intensity of the cry of despair that immediately takes the form of Divine care and compassion. . . . Do not think that there was a reply from the other side . . . because the dialogue 'goes on within each heart with or without words.'"¹⁴ Hussein and Askari on the cross can be seen as an example of the scriptural reasoning approach to how Muslims and Christians can read each other's sacred books by looking for parallels within their own that resonate with meaning without disputing the passage's authenticity or historical accuracy.

From In Search of Muḥammad to In Search of Jesus

Although I could have avoided discussing the crucifixion in my book on Muḥammad, I decided to touch on this because of its centrality to the enterprise and because I had already considered a number of other issues in Christian-Muslim relations. This brief treatment was in the context of my suggestion that Muḥammad could be an example and model for Christians especially in the realm of social ethics and social justice. In this context, it seemed appropriate to say something about the Muslim claim that can be seen as undermining and even denying the very foundations of Christian theology. Why would we give any credence to or imitate the example of someone who rejected what is fundamental to our convictions? I wanted to avoid juxtaposing a historical gospel account with a fictitious Qur'ānic version. Like Hussein, I focused on how Q4:156 might yield meaning that neither denies nor affirms the crucifixion. My suggestion was that rather than explicitly denying the cross, the passage rejects the attribution of blame to "the Jews" that resulted in the charge that Jews had killed God and in centuries of anti-Semitism and persecution. The "they slew him not"

13. Cragg, introduction to *City of Wrong*, 11–12.
14. Askari, *Alone to Alone*, 103.

refers to a claim that Jews killed Jesus. Blaming "Jews" for killing Jesus can be seen as a deliberate attempt to exonerate Pilate in an effort to court the favor of the Roman state. Given that Jesus and his disciples were Jews, the very term "the Jews" (who plotted to kill Jesus) creates an artificial distinction for purposes of vilification and polemic. This is an occasion when I do credit redaction criticism. My point is that blaming anyone other than ourselves, our own sins and those of all humans, for killing Jesus, is theologically suspect. Given the conviction that only Jesus' death could redeem humanity, that Jesus' death was necessary for human salvation, Christians should have thanked the Jews for doing us all an essential service. I wrote, "If Jesus' death was no accident, but part of God's redemptive plan, so that there was 'no other way,' . . . the blame rests with us all."[15] Human rebellion from Eden on, not the actions of one group of people or of one individual, killed Jesus. The intent of the rather dubious *Gospel of Judas*, too, is to redeem Judas from calumny since his "betrayal" of Jesus was a necessary part of the redemptive process.

In arguing that Q4:156 is correct in saying that "the Jews" did not kill Jesus, I also drew on Geoffrey Parrinder (1910–2005) and R. C. Zaehner (1913–1974), who saw a parallel here at Q8:17 when the Muslims were celebrating their victory at the Battle of Badr and taking all the credit. God sternly reminded them that "ye did not kill them but God" had.[16] Turning to my *In Search of Jesus*, I discovered, to my surprise, how some Christians and others share the widespread Muslim belief that Jesus did not die on the cross. This opened up for me the possibility that Christians can conceive of a Christianity without the cross playing such a fundamental role. Rather, for some, Jesus had children and died somewhere in France, or in India. Ahmadiyya Muslims, too, locate Jesus' tomb in Kashmir. Often, Jesus is portrayed as surviving the cross. For others he did die and the disciples faked the resurrection. Or, Paul is credited with inventing the myth of Jesus as a dying and rising, Son of God savior. Paul is fairly routinely depicted in Jewish and Muslim texts as the real inventor of Christian doctrines. In contrast, the real Jesus of history was a teacher who pointed his followers toward the One God, and demanded righteous conduct. He was fully human, not a divine figure which Paul invented. Scriptural passages that support ideas about a sacrificial death or a divine Jesus were inserted by later editors of the New Testament text. What Jesus requires of us is to do

---

15. Bennett, *In Search of Jesus*, 238–39.
16. Parrinder, *Jesus in the Qur'an*, 120; Zaehner, *At Sundry Times*, 212.

as he did, not to believe that we are redeemed by his blood. I have struggled with the idea that divine justice demanded or required a sinless sacrifice so that sin could be forgiven because the necessary price has been paid. Blood language does not fit comfortably with my conviction that God's love is strong enough to save without a price being paid. However, early Christian writers expressed their conviction that Jesus' life of love and his death—that refused to compromise with evil or to resist by force—were instruments of divine mercy by using notions and language that were available to them from first-century culture. This also drew on the Hebrew concept of blood sacrifice at, for example, Leviticus 17:11. I tend toward seeing the incarnation as the primary event—God re-sanctifying human life and the whole of creation by becoming a flesh-and-blood person in Jesus, or dwelling in Jesus in a unique way that challenges our ability to describe this reality. I see the *Gospel of Thomas*'s lack of a crucifixion narrative not only as a result of its style—a list of sayings rather than a chronological account of Jesus' life—but as indicating that for Thomas Christians the cross was not essential to their theology. That which is spiritual cannot die. Elaine Pagels, who sees Thomas's gospel as a rival for canonical status with John's, whose supporters triumphed, points out that the cross was not a Christian symbol for several centuries.[17] Personally, given how Jesus challenged those who exercised political and religious authority, how this should be exercised, how he condemned the values that perpetuated wealth and privilege, I think that Jesus was never destined to die a natural death. His only option to avoid the cross was violence, compromise, or retirement from preaching. He did none of these. By dying a cruel and undeserved death, Jesus set the standard of how, if confronted with evil, we must refuse to compromise even in the face of death. Our faith embraces the hope that the world will learn that injustice cannot win, which for us Jesus' resurrection guarantees. Jesus' whole life, from birth to death, set out the paradigm of sacrificial love that God requires us to imitate. I concluded my 2008 chapter as follows:

> By way of conclusion, put simply, perhaps we can reflect on whether the absence of the cross in Islam (or apparent absence of the Cross) must generate as much consternation among Christians as it has traditionally caused us.[18]

---

17. Pagels, *Beyond Belief*, 41.
18. Bennett, *Christian-Muslim Relations*, 175.

Recent Support from the Writing of Elizabeth Johnson: Concluding Observations

The weakness of my position described above lies in the rejoinder that Christian soteriology rests on Jesus' death as the necessary cost of human sin. Cragg refers to the cross as the "central theme of New Testament witness in the very genesis of the Church"[19] in his rejoinder to my chapter. Yet is the cross central to Jesus' message of love of God and neighbor, of feeding the hungry, liberating the oppressed, restoring justice, ending war, and sending the rich away empty? Is it essential for his summons to us to help heal the world's brokenness, to restore Eden, to reconcile all things with the Divine? Elizabeth A. Johnson (2018) not only finds emphasis on the cross in soteriological thought too concerned with human redemption to the exclusion of all created beings and the cosmos but argues that the theology of substitution was a late development. In *Creation and the Cross: The Mercy of God for a Planet in Peril*, Johnson credits the invention of what has dominated Christian theology for centuries, the doctrine that Jesus' death substituted for ours, to Anselm of Canterbury (1033–1109 CE). Scripture, she writes, "offers multiple ways of speaking about salvation and diverse ways of interpreting the Cross" and it was not until Anslem that "one way predominated."[20] After Anslem, most Christians have favored a "focus on sin and the cross" rather than on other understandings that instead emphasize "incarnation as redemptive of all creation" and the "resurrection of the Crucified as pledge of hope for all finite creatures who die."[21] Anselm's "satisfaction theory ... made it clear that Jesus' death paid back what was due to God because of the sins of human beings, allowing divine mercy to flow."[22] She traces this to medieval legal notions of the need for transgressions to be paid for so that respect for the feudal lord was maintained.[23]

Transferred to God, this demanded a payment in substitution for sin. "One must pay back for offences," or stand in contempt of "the Creator and an orderly cosmos."[24] "God," said Anselm, "maintains nothing with more

---

19. Cragg, "Qur'an and the Cross," 177.
20. Johnson, *Creation and the Cross*, xii.
21. Johnson, *Creation and the Cross*, xii.
22. Johnson, *Creation and the Cross*, xiii.
23. Johnson, *Creation and the Cross*, 4–5.
24. Johnson, *Creation and the Cross*, 5–6.

justice than the honor of his own dignity."[25] Throughout her book, framed as a dialogue following Anselm's style, Johnson critiques Anselm's theology. For Anselm, even if salvation could have been accomplished differently, "divine honor demanded that Jesus' death atone for human sin, save the human race, and open up the possibility of eternal happiness."[26] Anselm's satisfaction theory resulted in "patterns of spirituality that focused on the cross,"[27] eventually leading to all the blood language of classical hymns. Johnson prefers a "more holistic understanding of salvation,"[28] asking, "What if God neither needed nor wanted the cross in order to save the world from sin?"[29] "Unhitching divine mercy," she continued, "from the necessity of the cross does not necessarily leave people in their sins, but opens up a different way to re-establish relationship with God."[30] This resonates with my thought that the cross is not the mechanism of salvation but part of a larger salvific event represented by the whole of Jesus' life. Nor do I think that the cross was planned, although I do see Jesus' execution as inevitable given the life he lived, and I see profound meaning in his voluntary suffering which he could have avoided by walking a path that pleased instead of offending the powerful. Johnson says that an alternative theory needs to view God differently. God is not a feudal lord "in need of satisfaction, or an angry father, nor a punishing cosmic ruler"[31] but the Creator who "from the beginning" pours out "divine mercy to bring about a new creation."[32] This resonates with my often stated claim, in sermons, that divine love and mercy has no limit. She proposes a "theology of accompaniment" in which God always forgives sin from the depths of divine love and compassion without any price.[33] In Jesus, God came into our world to accompany us in the struggle to restore creation. Jesus' "brutal death" was not "to placate divine honor" but enacted "the solidarity of the gracious and merciful God with all who die and especially with victims of injustice, opening hope of resurrection amid the horror" (50). She cites many biblical passages that

---

25. Johnson, *Creation and the Cross*, 7.
26. Johnson, *Creation and the Cross*, 11.
27. Johnson, *Creation and the Cross*, 13.
28. Johnson, *Creation and the Cross*, 14.
29. Johnson, *Creation and the Cross*, 17.
30. Johnson, *Creation and the Cross*.
31. Johnson, *Creation and the Cross*, 46.
32. Johnson, *Creation and the Cross*, 47.
33. Johnson, *Creation and the Cross*, 50.

speak of the whole cosmos being restored to its original state. The figure of the servant in scripture tells of one who is chosen to "restore justice to the earth, or to heal bruises and restore righteousness."[34] For many Jews, this Servant is Israel herself.[35] Jesus can also be viewed as this Servant, whose mission was reconciliation, redemption, and self-giving. I agree with Johnson that Jesus did not understand his death in terms of "sacrifice or redemption" but that "in radical fidelity to God and in service of the people whom he loved, he stayed the course and was crucified to death." Later, the church interpolated language of substitution and atonement into "the way the story of Jesus was told" (89). The resurrection lifts Jesus from the finite realm of this world into one who partakes in "the omnipresence of God's own love."[36]

For Johnson, God's presence with Jesus through his life and death challenges the satisfaction theory that a debt needed to be paid for human sin because, since God accompanied Jesus on the cross, this would mean that God would have paid God's-self.[37] Instead of being part of a "masterplan in the divine mind to engineer" Jesus' death, the cross is an expression of God's solidarity with the human condition, a call for us to "bend every effort to stand with God in solidarity with those who suffer, and create situations where life can flourish," giving a "resurrecting world a foothold in this fractured world."[38] For Johnson, "interpreting the cross this way foregrounds the meaning of salvation as God's accompanying the whole troubled, sinful, agonized, and dying world into the depths of agony and death and beyond."[39] Referring also to points of agreement with Anselm, Johnson concludes with a citation that describes God's "merciful ways with the world as 'indescribably beautiful'" expressing "exceeding love and tenderness toward us" and the whole community of creation.[40]

---

34. Johnson, *Creation and the Cross*, 55.
35. Johnson, *Creation and the Cross*, 56.
36. Johnson, *Creation and the Cross*, 103.
37. Johnson, *Creation and the Cross*, 108.
38. Johnson, *Creation and the Cross*, 108.
39. Johnson, *Creation and the Cross*, 194.
40. Johnson, *Creation and the Cross*, 226.

Conclusion

Islam's rejection of the cross—or apparent rejection—is rooted in an understanding of salvation as God's free gift to humanity, the result of God's endless mercy. The satisfaction theology of salvation makes God's mercy contingent on a price being paid, and sees Jesus' death on the cross as paying this. Christian insistence on the need for a sinless sacrifice as a condition for human redemption flies in the face of Muslim conviction that salvation is unconditionally given. Denial that the crucifixion happened removes the ground from under Christian soteriology. It is almost certainly too ambitious to think that Christians will persuade Muslims that they are completely wrong about Jesus' death. Christians will continue to accept the crucifixion as historical fact while Muslims will see this a theological fiction. Yet, in my view, there can be a meeting halfway here. An understanding of the cross that removes it from the center while including it as part of a wider act of redemption, from incarnation to ascension, moves toward the Muslim view that Jesus' death on the cross was not essential for salvation. It also honors Christian belief that Jesus was crucified. There may be some possibility, perhaps, that Q4:156's ambiguous languages may result in some Muslims accepting that Jesus did die on the cross but was raised to life in vindication of his goodness. Just as Muḥammad's persecution and suffering at Mecca was vindicated by his success in Medina so Jesus' resurrection vindicated his death. In fact, the Qur'ān affirms that Jesus will be resurrected. For Muslims this is a future event. For Christians, it has already happened. What impresses me about Johnson's theology of accompaniment is how it embraces all creatures, and the cosmos itself, as objects of God's love, which God does not limit to the human race but extends universally to mend what we have spoiled and heal what we have hurt. In all the brokenness of creation, the planet and its nonhuman occupants are the innocent victims of our selfish choices. For her, Jesus' incarnation involved entering a relationship with all creatures, since we live in symbioses with creation: "Like a pebble thrown into a pond, the incarnation ripples outward with saving ramifications for all flesh, including flesh that is other than human."[41] This resonates with God's concern for all creatures in the Qur'ān, who have rights[42] and with how God will roll the world up like a scroll as it was initially unfolded (Q21:104), which some

---

41. Johnson, *Creation and the Cross*, 184.
42. See Bennett, *Interpreting the Qur'an*, 39, 60, 66.

see as the restoration of its original perfection. I have long found the idea of the natural world as a living organism attractive. We exist within and as part of this organism. We do not own the cosmos. Meant to help maintain its balance and harmony, we instead damage the ecosystem through greed and exploitation. Our divine calling is to partner with creation and Creator to bring about what Pierre Teilhard de Chardin (1881–1955), the French Jesuit thinker, called the Omega Point, the final unification of all life. I see some parallel here with the thought of the poet-philosopher Muhammad Iqbal (1877–1938), for whom the full potentiality of the divine will only be actualized when humanity assumes responsibility to "shape . . . the destiny of the universe, now by adjusting himself to its forces, now by putting the whole of his energy to mould its forces . . . and in this process of progressive change God becomes a co-worker with him, provided man takes the initiative."[43] For Iqbal, the Qur'ān "embodies an essentially dynamic outlook on life"[44] that requires reinterpretation in the light of progress, change, and discovery. The point of Jesus life, death, and resurrection was not primarily to allow us to enter heaven after death but to summons us to the great work of cosmic restoration, the reconciliation of all things (Col 1:20). We who are Christian or Muslim miss this if we spend too much time disputing the accuracy of the Bible's or Qur'ān's version of a single event in the story of Jesus. We may well benefit from listening to what Askari called our "complimentary witness on Jesus.[45]

---

43. Iqbal, *Reconstruction of Religious Thought*, 10.
44. Iqbal, *Reconstruction of Religious thought*, 118.
45. Askari, "Jesus in Islam," 146.

Chapter Five

The State of Official Church-Related Christian-Muslim Dialogue

How the Vatican and the World Council of Churches Paved the Way

MY personal journey in search of understanding Islam in relation to my faith as a Christian has largely taken place against the backdrop of dialogues sponsored by the Vatican, the World Council of Churches, and other Church agencies. This chapter sketches some of these initiatives. Obviously, Christians and Muslims meet in dialogue in many countries, but this book is primarily although not exclusively intended for readers in North America, so this survey focuses on the United States. However, dialogue initiatives in the United States, as elsewhere, have been stimulated by developments at the international level, the Vatican for Roman Catholics and the World Council of Churches (WCC) for Protestants and Orthodox. The Vatican II declaration *Nostra Aetate* (1965), stimulated by Rahner's thought, encouraged Catholic rethinking of attitudes toward Muslims and followers of other religions. Twenty-five years after *Nostra Aetate*, the Vatican published *Dialogue and Proclamation*, which identified four modes of dialogue, namely:

1. That of life in which we share "joys and sorrows," our "human problems and preoccupations" with each other.
2. That of action, in which we collaborated with each other for the "liberation of people."
3. That of theological exchange, where specialists share their beliefs and seek to better understand their own faith and that of others.

4. That of religious experience, where we share our spiritual riches and traditions of prayer (para. 42).

The document stresses the necessity of dialogue for social justice and human liberation, pointing out that if limited to the type of exchange at number 3 it will become a "domain reserved for specialists." Rather, encounter and dialogue should involve all members of the church so that it connects with daily life and opens up possibilities to cooperate "in promoting human and spiritual values" (para. 43).

Developments locally mirrored those at the global level; thus, when the Vatican and the World Council of Churches set up commissions or agencies for dialogue, respectively, in 1964 and 1971, this was reflected later by developments in the United States. Both world bodies have had name changes; for convenience they are referred to here as the Vatican and World Council of Churches' agencies. Both have staff specializing in Christian-Muslim relations and sponsor dialogue meetings. The Vatican body set up the Commission for Religious Relations with Muslims in 1974. The first WCC Christian-Muslim relations meeting took place in March 1969.[1] Syed Hasan Askari had taken part in WCC meetings before he joined the Selly Oak faculty. Kerr was also an early participant. These agencies partnered with their counterparts in the United States to sponsor various colloquia, seminars, and conferences. From the beginning, the Vatican and the WCC cooperated with each other. While the Catholic Church is not formally in membership with the WCC, at the committee and program level, Catholics are fully involved as equal participants.

Catholic-Muslim Dialogue in the United States

The United States Conference of Catholic Bishops Secretariat for Ecumenical and Interreligious Affairs (established 1964) has sponsored and participated in Christian-Muslim exchange, beginning in the late 1980s. Interreligious Affairs was added to the secretariat's remit in 1987. Its work has been informed by the Vatican's *Guidelines for Dialogue between Christians and Muslims*, edited by Maurice Bormans, originally published in 1970, revised in 1981. The WCC published *Issues in Christian-Muslim Relations: Ecumenical Considerations* in 1991. I was part of two working party meetings that drafted this document. What follows does not list

---

1. See Brown, *Meeting in Faith*, 3.

every initiative but illustrates that formalized Catholic-Muslim relations are well established, and healthy. For example, the Secretariat convened or co-convened a series of consultations on Christian-Muslim relations (1989, 1990, 1993) and a number of national Catholic-Muslim dialogues (two in 1991, one in 1992), of which the last two were co-planned with the American Muslim Council (AMC). The Catholic Bishops Conference and AMC released joint statements in 1993 after the World Trade Center bombing and in 1995 before the United Nations Conference on population and development. At the conference itself, which met in Cairo, Catholics and Muslims cooperated on a number of issues. The Catholic Bishops Conference has also held various consultations with Muslim experts on public policy (1995, 1996). In 1996, Cardinal Keeler of Baltimore and Imam W. D. Muhammad jointly led a visit to Rome. Also in 1996, a series of regional dialogues was launched cosponsored by Muslim organizations. The regions are the Mid-Atlantic, the Mid-West and the West Coast. Each is cochaired by a bishop and an official from the cosponsoring Muslim organization. They meet annually. Topics discussed range from marriage and family life, revelation and prayer, to peace and justice; a number of statements have been published. Especially involved from the Muslim community are the Islamic Society of North America (ISNA, founded 1981) and American Muslim Council (founded 1990). ISNA aims to build bridges between diverse elements within Islam, and with other religions outside Islam. The American Muslim Council's aims include fostering the common welfare of all people in the United States. In early 2016, the secretariat also established a national Catholic-Muslim Plenary.

The National Council of the Churches of Christ USA and Dialogue with Muslims

The NNCC (founded 1950) established a task force (later office) on Christian-Muslim relations in 1977, appointing Byron Haines (1928–1990), formerly a Presbyterian missionary in Pakistan, as director. Both Baines and his successor (from 1988), R. Marston Speight (1924–2011), formerly a United Methodist missionary in Algeria and Tunisia, operated from the Duncan Black Macdonald Center for Christian-Muslim Relations at Hartford Seminary, Connecticut (founded 1971). Speight translated the Catholic Guidelines into English (from the original French). The seminary, effectively an extension of the NCC's program, has attracted Muslim students to its courses, pioneering the training of Muslims for state-funded chaplaincy (in prisons, hospitals, and the armed services for which certified training is required). I first visited Hartford Seminary in April 1989. Since 1991, it has employed Muslim as well as Christian faculty following the precedent set by the Selly Oak Centre. The two institutions had close ties. A similar list of initiatives to those involving Catholics described above by the NCCC and by several of its thirty-seven member churches or communions would show that a formal mechanism for dialogue has now existed for many years involving mainly Protestants and Orthodox Christians. This writer attended one meeting, part of a regional series, in April 1989, at which topics such as prayer and fasting were discussed, but also what Muḥammad might mean for Christians, and what Jesus means for Muslims. The colloquium took place in Toronto, courtesy of the Canadian Council of Churches' interreligious desk, with Christian and Muslim participants from north and south of the border. Among Protestant denominations, the United Church of Christ's General Synod issued a brief statement on Christian-Muslim relations in 1989, calling on members to break down walls of racial, cultural, and religious division. Christians should "broaden their experience, revise attitudes and enrich theological perspectives of their faith in the context of Islam and the witness of Muslims" (UCC 1989). With other such statements, this one describes Islam as enjoying a special relationship with Judaism and Christianity as one of three Abrahamic faiths. I referred in my introduction to the 2003 statement by the Alliance of Baptists, the first from a Baptist body.

In 1991, when the NCCC's Interreligious Relations Commission was formed, Christian-Muslim relations (and also Christian-Jewish relations, which began in 1973 as an office) was transferred to its remit. In 2014, the council underwent a restructuring that replaced commissions with new convening tables. In addition to forming the Convening Table on Interreligious Relations and Collaboration on Topics of Mutual Concern, to which I was named, the council declared interreligious relations with a focus on peacemaking as a priority in all its work. The other priority addresses the issue of mass incarceration.

The National Muslim Christian Initiative (NMCI) began in March 2008, cosponsored by NCCC and the Islamic Society of North America, to "enhance mutual understanding, respect, appreciation and support of what is sacred for each other through dialogue education sustained visible encounters that foster and nurture relationships." Topics discussed at meetings include Abraham and Our Respective Scriptures; Islamophobia generally; more specifically, Negative Instances of Anti-Muslim Sentiment, Bigotry and Hate Crimes in the United States, and Constructive Collaboration to Respond to These; the Meaning of Terrorism; Christian Persecution in the Middle East; Challenges from the Left and Right in Our Communities; and the Intersection of Religious Freedom and Respect for What Others Hold Sacred. At our most recent meeting, February 12, 2019, we discussed our experiences of, concerns with and response to racism and immigration today. Since 2014, the US Council of Muslim Organizations has cosponsored the NCMI.

The mature relationship between the NCCC and ISNA saw the latter's national interreligious director, Sayyid M. Syeed, bringing greetings to the reconstituted NCCC's first Christian Unity Gathering in May 2014, when he stated that he believed in "the Trinity," that is, in friendship and cooperation between NCCC, ISNA, and the Union for Reform Judaism, which also presented greetings. Recent meetings, which I have attended, have seen the Islamic Circle of North America (founded 1968) and the Council of Muslim Organizations (founded 2014) as cosponsors, with participation also by the Council on American Islamic Relations (founded 1994).

A Baptist Initiative

Another post 9/11 development is a Baptist Muslim dialogue initiated in response to the *A Common Word* program launched by the Royal House of Jordan. On October 13, 2007, signed by 138 Muslim scholars and intellectuals, this open letter was addressed and sent to twenty-seven named Christian leaders, and to "leaders of Christian churches everywhere." It generated responses from individuals, churches, and from specially convened conferences. *ACW* (the title is derived from Q3:64) seeks to promote dialogue around love of God and love of neighbor, obligatory for all three Abrahamic faiths. It posits that without peace between Christians and Muslims, world peace is beyond reach.

Citing Qur'an 5:34, it suggests that competition in peacemaking, "righteousness and good works" should replace conflict between the two religions. Sponsored by the King of Jordan, a postmodernist analysis of this initiative would identify various geopolitical issues and bids to take the lead in defining Islam and its role in the world, involving competition between various regional actors such as Saudi Arabia. Leaving such issues aside, *ACW* had, in the words of the then Archbishop of Canterbury Rowan Williams, a "unique role in stimulating discussion at the deepest level across the world."[2] *ACW* builds on an earlier open letter to Pope Benedict XVI (October 13, 2006) following his University of Regensburg address of September 12, 2007 (which mentioned allegations about Islam as violent and irrational), and on the Amman Interfaith Message (July 2005), itself related to the *Amman Message* (2004), calling for intra-Muslim harmony. Many responses were published in the fifth-anniversary edition. These include those from the Evangelical Lutheran Church in America,[3] from three hundred Christian scholars and leaders organized by Yale University in October 2007, "the first broad-based Christian response,"[4] and an account of the subsequent Yale sponsored conference in July 2008 attended by seventy Muslims, seventy Christian, and seven Jewish guests.[5] At the 2008 Yale conference, addressed by then senator John Kerry (later secretary of state), Christian participants crossed denominational boundaries. The fifth-anniversary edition also commented on the involvement of evangelicals, including Robert Schuller of the Crystal Cathedral and Leith Anderson, then president of the National Association of Evangelicals, as a breakthrough in Christian-Muslim relations.[6] Evangelicals do not usually take part in interreligious dialogue, and some who attended the Yale conference have had to respond to criticism. Anderson had to clarify that he had signed the statement in his private capacity, although he was listed as NAE president.[7] Critics reject the idea that Christians and Muslims worship the same God, a claim to which I referred above.[8] The Catholic Bishops Conference responded to *ACW* on October 13, 2007, NCCC on October 8, 2008. Internationally, *ACW* led to the formation of the Catholic-Muslim Forum. This first met in Rome, addressed by Pope Benedict[9] on November 4-6, 2008, then in Jordan, November 21-24, 2011, at the place held to have been Jesus' baptismal site (it will meet triannually), producing two

---

2. *Common Word*, 7.
3. *Common Word*, 137-38.
4. *Common Word*, 24.
5. *Common Word*, 25-27.
6. *Common Word*, 26.
7. *Common Word*, 28.
8. *Common Word*, 27.
9. This address is reproduced in *Common Word*, 237-40.

declarations by the time of writing.[10] Both declarations make various theological statements about divine love; they also call for action to advance humanity's common good through ending oppression, terrorism, and violent aggression. In the United States, *ACW* prompted another new initiative by a coalition of Baptists.

During 2007, Roy Medley, then general secretary of American Baptist Churches-USA, commented that, in the context of promoting intra-Baptist unity, perhaps dialogue with Islam might follow. He acknowledged the damage that hurtful statements by Baptists caused and that, given their historic commitment to religious freedom, proposed that Baptists should "respect other religions."[11] In fact, the first ever plea for complete religious liberty in English, by Baptist Thomas Helwys (1550–1616), included "Turks" (then synonymous with Muslim).[12] Visiting Baptists in Lebanon and Georgia in 2006 and 2007, Medley had been encouraged to help improve Baptist-Muslims relations. Following Medley's remarks, Sayyid M. Syeed wrote suggesting a conference. Subsequently, Syeed spoke at the American Baptist Churches' biennial gathering, the first Muslim to do so, and Medley spoke at ISNA's annual meeting. In January 2008, representatives of several Baptist conventions, including the Alliance, met in Hartford, where they launched the national Baptist-Muslim dialogue, which first met at Andover Newton Theological School in Boston in January 2009. Responding to *ACW* was a main aim. The first summit agreed a "Statement of Our Common Will" repudiating stereotypes and prejudice, encouraging cooperation, and launched a film project, *Different Books, Common Word: Baptists and Muslims*, released in 2010, which I describe in my next chapter. The second Baptist-Muslim summit took place in November 2012. Another meeting was held in April 2013 shortly after the Boston Bombing, when better understanding and greater respect was emphasized as even more urgent. More recently, the Baptist-Muslim Dialogue met in April 2018. The Alliance affiliated Baptist Seminary of the West gave space to Zaytuna College, an Islamic institution, on its campus (2010–2012). After Zaytuna moved into its own nearby premises it has maintained good relations with the seminary.

Parallel to this development in the United States, the Baptist World Alliance (BWA), whose former president, David Coffey, was a named

---

10. *Common Word*, 245–48, 249.
11. Kaylor, "American Muslim, Baptist Leaders."
12. See Bennett, "Thomas Helwys."

addressee of *ACW*, followed Coffey's initial brief response (October 16, 2007) with a detailed statement (December 26, 2008) (reproduced in *ACW* 2012: 213–34). One of the main authors was Paul Fiddes, BWA's Doctrine Commission chair, a full professor in Oxford's Theology Faculty. The response, which has extensive Qur'ān citations, drew on discussion at a BWA meeting in Prague (July 2008), where representatives of sixty-six Baptist conventions met, including "from areas of the world" experiencing "distressing religious conflicts." It also drew on written submissions from across the Baptist world. The document[13] affirmed that the "Common Word" shared by Baptists and Muslims around love of God and of neighbor also represents "common ground," which is not only a "strategy for dialogue, but a gift of God to us all." Remarking on Baptists' commitment to religious freedom, which it calls "an imperative," the document ends with a call for grassroots engagement, "to change attitudes and prejudices." It also encouraged joint study of the Bible and of the Qur'ān. This overlaps with an initiative known as *scriptural reasoning*, which for the past fifteen years or so has seen small circles of Jews, Christians, and Muslims gather to study each other's scriptures. I will return to scriptural reasoning in my next chapter. I first encountered scriptural reasoning while teaching for the University of Cambridge Interfaith Programme's first summer school in July 2011 (funded by the Sultan of Oman). After responding to *ACW*, the BWA set up a commission to provide space for shared reflection on Baptist-Muslim relations in order to develop mutual respect, promote security, peace, and common welfare between Baptists and their Muslim sisters and brothers.

A Joint WCC, Vatican, and World Evangelical Alliance Initiative

Finally, while interfaith dialogue is usually associated with the ecumenical movement, in 2011 the WCC, the Vatican, and the World Evangelical Alliance jointly published *Christian Witness in a Multi-Religious World: Recommendations for Conduct*. This important document resulted from a five year conversation. While affirming that witnessing our faith is a biblically mandated duty, the document called for the rejection of disrespectful, violent and coercive methods of evangelism. We should "build relationships of

---

13. See "Baptist World Alliance Responds to Muslim Letter," *A Common Word*, January 8, 2009, https://www.acommonword.com/baptist-world-alliance-responds-to-muslim-letter.

respect and trust with people of different religions so as to facilitate deeper understanding, reconciliation and cooperation for the common good." The document recommends that, where possible, guidelines for the conduct of Christian witness should be formulated "ecumenically, and in consultation with representatives of other religions." The section on principles gives biblical references for each. Another recommendation states that "dialogue can provide new opportunities for resolving conflicts, restoring justice, healing of memories, reconciliation and peace-building," especially in contexts "where years of tension and conflict have created deep suspicions and breaches of trust between communities," which describes Christian-Muslim relations only too accurately. In February 2019, Pope Francis and the Grand Imam of Al-Azhar signed a document on human fraternity and living together for world peace in Abu Dhabi during the Human Fraternity Meeting. The declaration calls on "all concerned to stop using religions to incite hatred, violence, extremism, and blind fanaticism, and to refrain from using the name of God to justify acts of murder, exile, terrorism, and oppression." It invites Christians and Muslims to make the document "the object of research and reflection in all schools, universities and institutes of formation."[14]

Conclusion

In the United States and elsewhere, 9/11 and subsequent acts of terror by self-defined Muslims reinforced many negative tropes about Islam and Muslims. Both are seen as incompatible with "our values" and "our security" even as a threat to our very "way of life." However, as the above survey of dialogue initiative shows, many Christians have reached out in solidarity to their Muslim neighbors so much so that the NCCC's membership is out of step with popular opinion. Recent days have seen an increase of violence toward Muslims (127 reported incidents in 2016).[15] A January 2017 Pew Research poll asked respondents to rate, on a thermometer-like scale of 0–100, with 0 representing the most negative feelings, how they viewed Muslims. The result was 48 degrees.[16] Although this was eight degrees

---

14. See "Apostolic Journey of His Holiness Pope Francis to the United Arab Emirates (3–5 February 2019)," https://w2.vatican.va/content/francesco/en/travels/2019/outside/documents/papa-francesco_20190204_documento-fratellanza-umana.html.

15. See Kishi, "Assaults against Muslims."

16. See Pew, "U.S. Muslims Concerned."

warmer than when this question was first asked in 2014 it still indicates a high level of suspicion and dislike. Encouragingly, however, Pew also reported, July 26, 2017, that "a large—and growing—majority of the public says that Muslims in the United States face a lot of discrimination, while roughly half of US adults say media coverage of Muslims is unfair." My next chapter looks at how Christians and Christian congregations might counter negative tropes and partner with their Muslim neighbors.

Chapter Six

Suggestions on How Christians Can Challenge Negative Tropes about Muslims and Cooperate in Peace and Justice Advocacy, Social and Community Development

The Roots of Islamophobia

THIS chapter begins by tracing the development of Islamophobia in the West. This has reinforced negative tropes about Islam and Muslims. After critiquing media coverage, resources that can help us to become better informed are described and recommended. These include documentaries, a novel, and a film. My focus will be on how Islamophobia has impacted the lives of Muslims, and also of others who are mistakenly identified as Muslim, in the United States. Convinced that not bearing false witness against our neighbors is a Christian duty, my aim is to encourage us to stand "shoulder to shoulder" with Muslims in the face of hostility and suspicion. Whatever we might think about the spiritual status of individuals who are Muslim, their demonization dehumanizes them in ways that challenge us to defend their right to live free from prejudice. The NCCC supports the Shoulder to Shoulder Campaign, which regards pluralism, religious freedom, and mutual respect as foundational American values which should be proactively affirmed by all of us. For some, though, even expressions of solidarity are controversial. At the 2016 NCCC Christian Unity Gathering, a small number objected to a group photograph of delegates in front of a sign saying "we stand with our Muslim neighbors" because they saw this as this betraying Christian minorities elsewhere who are ill-treated by Muslims. I also suggest ideas that Christians interested in forming partnerships with Muslims in social action, community development, peace and justice advocacy can consider. I begin with how world events and some closer to home have fueled the development of Islamophobia. This is defined as dislike, fear of, or prejudice against Islam, especially when allied with political ideologies. The report, *Islamophobia: A Challenge for Us All*, published by the Runnymede Trust in Britain in 1997, popularized the term. During my initial year at Selly Oak, the Islamic Revolution in Iran toppled the Shah, and sixty American citizens were taken hostage at the US Embassy. They remained in captivity until January 21, 1981, four hundred forty-four days later, while I was working in Bangladesh. Known as the Iranian hostage crisis, this event brought political Islam to the West's attention and changed the dynamic of the Middle East. Until this event, I cannot recall Islam attracting very much public or media attention. This soon changed. Some friends had even expressed skepticism that there was much mileage in my choice of Islam as an academic specialism. Even in preparation for missionary work in Bangladesh with the traditional aim of gaining Christian converts, given that most Christians there have Hindu and animist backgrounds, the study of Islam could seem irrelevant since any new converts were much more likely to be from Hindu or animist backgrounds. After this, however, people commented on how timely my decision to focus on Islam had been. The United States and Israel both lost an ally in the region, which they now regard as a foe. Academically, the Islamic Revolution gave some impetus to the study of Islam which also began to attract the interest of scholars working in political science and international affairs. My Islam: An Introduction course at New Paltz (REL275), which I designed, is cross listed with international relations. Scholars realized that Islamic-inspired movements were players in the political sphere. Until then, Islam was widely perceived in the West as a spent force. Since the demise of the Ottoman Empire, no Muslim state represented a serious military or economic threat to the rest of the world. Iran's project of exporting the revolution could now be seen as a danger to world stability. Iran now challenged the United States' role in the Middle East. Well-established Sunni movements such as the Muslim Brotherhood also took encouragement from Iran's revolution, even though they are hostile toward Iran's version of Islam. Most such movements reject the Islamic authenticity of monarchies and secular states in the Muslim world and oppose such regimes. These kingdoms, emirates, and states happen to be allied with the United States. So was Iraq during the Iraq-Iran war (1980–1988). As I continued to engage with Islam and Muslims, initially in Bangladesh and later with the Muslim communities in Britain and in the United States, I experienced a perceptible increase in hostility toward Islam among the non-Muslim majority.

A series of events made it possible for some to represent Islam as a problem that had to be dealt with. For some, this has a strong religious component; Islam is a false faith that rejects Christ, encourages violence, and denies civil rights. For others, Islam is viewed more in political terms as a threat to the world order, especially to the West's stability and security. Inevitably, negative tropes about Muslims have impacted those who live in Europe and North America. In earlier centuries, many of the same tropes were widespread but the Other that these created lived a long way off. Now, European and North American Muslims are our fellow citizens. Negative tropes transform them into the Other in our midst. Muslims fought for the Republic in the Revolutionary War and have lived here since colonial times, yet these Others in the United States are seen as outsiders who do not properly belong. Their presence is considered dangerous. Fear of Islam in the West also has a political component that dates from 1991 when the Cold War ended, an event that has no obvious Islamic element. However, soon after this some began to represent Islam as the "Green Threat" that had replaced the "Red Threat," almost certainly rooted in the psychological need to focus on an actual or perceived enemy. John L. Esposito wrote about this in an important and perceptive article, "Islam and the West: Beyond the Green Menace" (1994). A year earlier, a *Foreign Affairs* article by Harvard's Samuel P. Huntington, called "The Class of Civilization" (1993), claimed that Muslim-majority states have "bloody borders"[1] and predicted that the next global clash would be between a Muslim-neo-Confucian alliance and the rest of the world. In his view, Islam's absolutist claims and agenda makes peaceful coexistence with other religions and civilizations impossible. One result of this thesis was a United Nations-supported initiative, first proposed by Iran's President Khatami, called the Dialogue of Civilizations, launched in 2001 to counter Huntington's alarmist view. The stigmatizing of Muslims as perpetrators of violence actually flies in the face of their minimal or non-involvement in many twentieth-century conflicts, such as World War II, the Korea and Vietnam Wars, and the fact that, this century, Muslim-majority states have been invaded by the United States and its allies. Muslims point out that they are often victims of violence and that this attracts little or no media attention. Currently, Muslims in

---

1. Huntington, "Clash of Civilizations?," 34.

Myanmar and China are being brutally victimized, which the media does mention, but internationally not much is being done to aid these victims.

Since I began my journey into Christian-Muslim encounter four decades ago, events that have fed Islamophobia include the Salman Rushdie affair (which began with the publication of *The Satanic Verses* in 1988), the Iraqi invasion of Kuwait, a US ally, in August 1990, which led to the Gulf War (August 2, 1990–February 28, 1991), the February 26, 1993, attack on the Twin Towers in New York and other attacks on US targets, including simultaneous attacks on the US Embassy in Nairobi and Dar-as-Salaam August 7, 1988, and on the *USS Cole* in Yemen (October 12, 2000). Listing everything would make the list too long but there is little doubt that the attack on the Twin Towers (September 11, 2001), which caused 2,996 fatalities, has had the biggest negative impact on how Muslims are perceived. In the film, described below, *My Name Is Khan* (2010), the main character says, "In the western world, history is marked simply by BC and AD. But now, there is at third distinction, 9/11." For readers here in the United States, Khaled A. Beydoun's *American Islamophobia* (2019) provides an up-to-date analysis of the roots and rise of fear of Islam and Muslims that argues that Islamophobia is actually a state-authorized and executed policy that "enlists private citizens to partake in the national project of identifying and punishing individuals stereotyped as presumptive terrorists."[2]

These attacks were carried out by operatives or associates of Al-Qaeda, an organization founded in 1988 to recruit volunteers in the fight against Soviet occupation of Afghanistan, but which also called for what it sees as a defensive war against the West generally and the United States in particular, which it claims are engaged in a crusade to destroy the Muslim world. While this represents an extreme view, there are far less extreme Muslims who call for a restructuring of the world order. The Egyptian feminist writer Nawal el Saadawi has written about "development" as "just another word for neo-colonialism." The word *aid*, she says, "can be just as deceiving."[3] As long as the global economic system is controlled by the North and operated for its benefits, the South, including Muslim-majority states, will remain poor. She calls for fair trade rather than charity, "Charity and injustice are two faces of the same coin."[4] Real equality between states would end injustice and make charity unnecessary. During the hostage crisis in Bangladesh, I witnessed

---

2. Beydoun, *American Islamophobia*, 90.
3. Saadawi, *Nawal El Saadawi Reader*, 13.
4. Saadawi, *Nawal El Saadawi Reader*, 13.

considerable anti-American sentiment fueled by the belief that the United States' policies serve American interests which help to keep Bangladesh as a bottomless "basket case" for aid, to cite former US secretary of state Henry Kissinger.[5] Others distrust the United States for being a friend one day and not the next; for example, the United States supported the *mujahidin* in Afghanistan when they fought the Soviet Union but turned against them after 9/11. The United States extols democracy yet has allied itself with absolute monarchs and totalitarian rulers in the Arab world when commercial and other interests take priority over principles.

Following 9/11, on October 7, 2001, the United States invaded Afghanistan to punish the Taliban for harboring Al-Qaeda's founder, Osama bin Laden; then the United States invaded Iraq on March 20, 2003, although there was no link between its dictatorial regime and the 9/11 attack. With the capture and execution of Bin Laden on May 20, 2011, Al-Qaeda, though still active, became less of a priority in the "War on Terror" launched by the United States after 9/11. Attention shifted to an offshoot, the Islamic State in Iraq and Syria (ISIS), which, as does Al-Qaeda, aims to reestablish the caliphate. Recent acts of terror in the United States and elsewhere in the West, carried out by self-defined Muslims routinely referred to as radical Islamic terrorists, were inspired by the Islamic State. Current US engagement in ongoing conflicts within the Muslim world, together with civil war in Yemen, Libya, and Syria, and the failure of such states as Somalia and Sudan, easily feed the perception that the Muslim world is a dangerous, unstable, lawless, and violent space. This trope lies behind Donald Trump's recent ban on visitors to the United States from seven Muslim-majority states and calls for a registry of Muslims in the United States.

How the Media Perpetuates Negative Tropes

In his *Covering Islam: How the Media and the Experts Determine How We See the Rest of the World* (revised ed., 1997), Edward Said wrote that "malicious generalizations about Islam have become the last acceptable form of denigration of foreign culture."[6] Earlier, Rana Kabbani wrote that "Western culture remains permeated with anti-Islamic reference." "Today's media coverage," she says "carries echoes of Medieval polemic."[7] She recounts how,

5. Hitchens, *Trial of Henry Kissinger*, 50.
6. Said, *Covering Islam*, xii.
7. Kabbani, *Letter to Christendom*, 9.

when she read a *Vanity Fair* interview of herself, she failed to recognize anything she had said. The article presented "a catalogue of horrors about Islam." Ahdaf Soueif's novel *The Map of Love* (1999), set in Egypt, depicts how one of her characters reacted when she heard that an American reporter wanted to meet her:

> Amal could not pretend that she was not wary. Wary and weary in advance: an American woman—a journalist . . . she braced herself: the fundamentalists, the veil, the cold peace, polygamy, women's status in Islam, female genital mutilation—which would it be?[8]

The issues identified in this quotation continue to attract media attention. The media depicts wearing the veil as a symbol of Muslim women's oppression and acts of terror by relatively few self-defined Muslims from the global population of 1.6 billion as if most Muslims condone, support or would carry out such acts themselves. The words "terrorist" and "Muslim" have been conflated. Words such as *jihād* and *fatwā*, which is often followed by "against," are repeatedly used even by so-called experts with little recognition of how Muslims understand these terms. Some Muslims do claim that present global circumstances permit acts of war and of what the media calls terror and speak of being involved in a total war, that is, since the West is corporately engaged in an anti-Muslim crusade there is no valid distinction between combatants and civilians as legitimate targets. Many Muslims, however, see these as aggressive acts that do not meet the criteria for armed *jihād* that resemble those of Just War theory, and point to classical rules of engagement that prohibit killing noncombatants, animals and destroying crops. They cite the tradition, attributed to the Prophet, that armed *jihād* is the lesser struggle while the greater struggle is the spiritual battle within Muslims to overcome their shortcomings and external striving to do good in the world. *Jihād* means to strive or struggle. It is not used—explicitly—in the Qur'ān for war, which uses *harb*. The armed *jihad* was classically regarded as a collective duty, organized by the state, which recruited participants. It was not as an individual duty. Constant media reference to *jihād* as holy war, and to individuals who volunteer with ISIS or other militant groups as jihadists, is misleading. The word *fatwā* entered popular vocabulary with Ayatollah Khomeini's opinion that Rushdie and those who published his novel were "condemned to death." While a *fatwā* is a nonbinding legal opinion, it was reported as if it was a judicial sentence.

---

8. Soueif, *Map of Love*, 6.

Habitually described as the *fatwā against* Rushdie, countless people think that *fatāwā* are always against something, whereas they can also permit acts such as blood or organ donation. Even though some Muslims acted on Khomeini's *fatwā* by killing translators and others involved in publishing, distributing, and translating the novel, many Muslims regarded the *fatwā* as invalid (it did not, in fact, follow the standard protocols).

Not everyone who speaks in response to events linked with Islam whom the media labels as an expert offer informed or unbiased commentary. Some people have established reputations as experts who have little real knowledge so that they can pursue their own agendas. Some possess credible qualifications but are biased. The Muslim Public Affairs Council describes Daniel Pipes, who has a Harvard doctorate in medieval Islamic history, for example, as a media darling who is "NOT an objective source on the issue of Islam, Muslims, American Muslims, or Israel/Palestine, and has demonstrated this time and time again."[9] He cites statistics on the American Muslim community that support his thesis that they represent a danger to the United States, intending to "take over" and establish *Shariāh* law and that the majority of Muslim institutes have been infiltrated by extremists. Bernard Lewis (1916–2018) had impressive academic credentials and made regular media appearances. However, an obituary described him as providing politicians with intellectual support for "bigotry and war in the Middle East,"

> Lewis was intellectually a towering figure. This meant he had the ability to do great good. Instead, he became the intellectual high priest for the calamitous wars which have caused such bloodshed across the Middle East, while doing unlimited damage to the standing of the United States.[10]

For example, soon after 9/11 he began to agitate for Saddam Hussein's ouster, although he later claimed to have opposed the invasion of Iraq. Reportedly, he told Vice President Dick Cheney: "I believe that one of the things you've got to do to Arabs is hit them between the eyes with a big stick" because "they respect power." He had written of a "clash of civilizations" before Huntington in a 1990 article, "The Roots of Muslim Rage"[11] to represent the Muslim world as engaged in a battle for survival with the

9. "The Truth about Daniel Pipes," https://www.mpac.org/programs/anti-terrorism-campaign/the-truth-about-daniel-pipes.php.
10. Oborne, "Do Not Weep."
11. Lewis, "Roots of Muslim Rage," 60.

West, and he referred to Muslims as if they all think and act identically. I have spoken about a double standard that demonizes all Muslims due to the arguably deviant actions of a few, while similar atrocities carried out by Christians are described without associating all Christians with these. The religious identity of non-Muslim mass killers goes unreported. This is what Reginald Bosworth Smith meant by turning the mirror upon ourselves. I dislike the term "Muslim terrorist." My personal view is that those who carry out atrocities disqualify themselves as Muslim. We do not hear white nationalist terrorists called "Christian terrorists" although many of them self-define as Christian. Such acts are also rarely described as terrorism. Thus,

> if a Muslim man planted bombs in predominately white neighborhoods before blowing himself up, you could bet that the White House and various media outlets would label him a terrorist and draw some connection between his religion and his violent acts. But the case of the Austin bomber reveals an enduring double standard: white Christian terrorists continue to get a free pass.[12]

I was with Zaki Badawi once when he received a call from the BBC to appear on a panel talking about the current Islam-related issue. He asked who else would participate. The answer was that they intended to invite a bishop. However, they could not say who it would be. Zaki commented that it seemed as if any bishop would suffice, regardless of their understanding of the topic under discussion, as long as they were seen to represent the established church. A misrepresentation that I have pointed out is the allegation that Muslims are slow to condemn acts of violence. Margaret Thatcher made this claim in October 2001, saying that too few Muslims had spoken out against the 9/11 atrocity. A few days later, the *Guardian*, where her remarks had appeared, published an article that referred to such Muslim responses as Zaki Badawi's joint statement with the archbishops of Canterbury and Westminster and the chief rabbi dated prior to her claim. In 2005, I described a number of important statements by influential Muslims rejecting that either Al-Qaeda or the 9/11 terrorists represented Islam.[13] Another issue is how, when Muslims express opposition to US foreign policy or to military action, they are accused of being un-American. This shuts down legitimate public debate about important issues on which many non-Muslims share their opinions. Writing in 2004, my friend Ziauddin

---

12. Camacho, "Why Mark Anthony Conditt."
13. Bennett, *Muslims and Modernity*, 226–27.

Sarder pointed out how post 9/11 Muslims have been reduced to two kinds: either they are terrorists at war with the West or "a liberal apologist who claims to be liberal and defend Islam as a peaceful religion.[14] This makes it all but impossible for Muslims to affirm American values on the one hand while they oppose US policy on the other hand. Books by the director of Jihad Watch, Robert Spencer, who self-promotes as an expert on radical Islam, reach a wide readership. Their titles alone, which include *The Truth about Muhammad, Founder of the World's Most Intolerant Religion* (2006) and *Not Peace but a Sword: The Great Chasm between Christianity and Islam* (2013), suggest their animus toward Islam. Even though the first of these texts made the prestigious *New York Times* bestseller list they should be avoided. Too much reporting fails to deal with Islam's heterogeneity as it is lived and practiced in almost fifty Muslim-majority states. For example, there are states where women's dress is policed and states where no dress codes are legally enforced. The actual status of women varies considerably and cannot be reduced to the stereotype of second-class citizenship. Five have had women prime ministers (Bangladesh, 2; Pakistan, 1; Mali, 1; Senegal, 2; and Turkey, 1) while Indonesia and Kyrgyzstan have each had a woman president, which flies in the face of the popular trope of the oppressed Muslim woman. It is difficult to conceive that a head of government is being oppressed.

Positive Media Representation

In response to negative and ill-informed media reporting, a number of independent documentaries, often broadcast by public television channels (PBS), offer alternative coverage. As Christians, we should try to filter out coverage that is recognizably biased or inaccurate in favor of the type of media productions described below. The Shoulder to Shoulder Campaign's *Toolkit for Mobilizing to Protect and Support American Muslims* (an evolving internet resource) encourages us to educate ourselves about Islam and American Muslims. The *Toolkit* also advises us not to rely on the news for our information. This will only give "a tiny fragment of the story." The production of material that seeks to tell the story from the Muslim perspective is a type of "writing back." Unless Muslims and their allies write about the American Muslim experience, others will do this for them and depict Muslims as disloyal and un-American, and that narrative

---

14. Sarder, *Desperately Seeking Paradise*, 51.

will become dominant. One excellent resource that I highly recommend, *American Muslims*, published by the US State Department, implicitly challenges negative and inaccurate images. *American Muslims* briefly surveys the history of Muslims in what is now the United States, chronicles Muslim achievements in politics, the judiciary, and other arenas, including entertainment and the arts. It emphasizes the racial diversity of the American Muslim community and how Muslims contribute to society through voluntary service and humanitarian work as well as in professional roles. Examples of community initiatives described include the 2009 campaign to devote one thousand days of service with 90 percent of projects carried out in cooperation with other faith communities and Chicago's Inner City Muslim Action Network which runs a no-cost health clinic. Many mosques run soup kitchens and other social programs. The largest Muslim community comprises African Americans, some of whom are descended from "Muslims who were brought to America centuries ago as slaves."[15] Nowhere else have Muslims "established one community with so much diversity"[16] despite the stereotypical image of Muslims as Arabs. Muslims are among the best educated, "entrepreneurial and hard-working faith communities in the USA."[17] They are "more likely than the average American to have an advanced degree."[18] Over the years of teaching here in the United States, I have had many Muslim students who went on to gain postgraduate degrees, often in medicine. About 10 percent of all physicians in the United States are Muslim. One, a cardiologist, recently helped to save my life. The document reports 2,100 Muslim congregations and 2.6 million adherents in 592 counties.[19] Some suggest that the number of Muslims is closer to seven million. Many Muslims identify with their countries of origin and with the United States without seeing any contradiction.[20] It is easy to overlook the contribution of Muslims to all branches of military services in the United States, which I described in a 2010 encyclopedia entry[21]. Use of American Muslims rather than Muslims in America recognizes that Muslims are as American as members of any other community, not merely people who

---

15. US Dept. of State, *American Muslims*, 24.
16. US Dept. of State, *American Muslims*, 34.
17. US Dept. of State, *American Muslims*, 25.
18. US Dept. of State, *American Muslims*, 25.
19. US Dept. of State, *American Muslims*, 25.
20. US Dept. of State, *American Muslims*, 26.
21. Bennett, "US Military."

reside here without really belonging. On the other hand, as I discuss below, post 9/11, however loyal Muslims are to the United States, others make it difficult for them to feel that they are fully accepted, and not viewed with suspicion. Looking at certain populations with suspicion has a lengthy history in the United States. Catholics, especially from Ireland and Italy, were perceived to be inauthentically American. The KKK was as anti-Catholic as it was anti-black and anti-Jewish. John F. Kennedy had to apologize for and defend his Catholic identity when he ran for the presidency. Many, misled by the labeling of Barack Obama as a Muslim, thought that this should preclude him from being elected to the presidency as recently as 2007. Of course, Donald Trump and others said that he was born in Africa so could not become president, who must be a natural-born citizen. Yet Muslims have fought and died for the United States, including in Iraq and Afghanistan. They have won military honors. *American Muslims* may at times go too far in the other direction. For example, it tends to minimize differences within the Muslim community that challenges describing it as "one." At the NCCC, we have experienced rivalry between ISNA and ICNA, with the former playing less of a role in our dialogues since the latter became more involved. On the other hand, these two organizations have spoken about merging for many years. Of course, Christians have no cause to brag about unity, which eludes us. The State Department's *Being Muslim in America* is also well worth reading.

Several resources respond to the demonization of Muslims in post-9/11 America. One of these, *Muhammad: The Legacy of a Prophet*, was produced by Alexander Kronemer and Michael Wolfe of Unity Productions Foundation for PBS in 2002. Promoted by the NCCC, and other interfaith organizations, this film presents interviews with Muslims in their homes, places of work and of worship and commentary by distinguished and empathetic non-Muslim scholars. It also narrates the life of Muḥammad and explores how American Muslims look to his example as they live as Muslims in the United States. In one scene, a man training for the Catholic diaconate visits a soup kitchen run by a mosque, where he tells a Muslim that he was unaware that such service was "even part of your creed."[22] Muslims interviewed include a FDNY fire marshal, a nurse, an artist, and many others. Daisy Khan speaks about her search for identity as a Muslim woman living in the United States as she worked out how to deal with the dominant culture, which for her led to rethinking some interpretations of Islam.

---

22. *Muhammad: Legacy of a Prophet*, script, 33.

Some of my Muslim students have spoken of how they want to practice Islam but not in the culturally conditioned form their parents experienced in Pakistan or elsewhere. Many feel comfortable wearing Western clothes, for example, even though some parents think that this is un-Islamic. Now executive director of the Women's Islamic Initiative for Spirituality and Equality (WISE), Khan once worked in the Twin Towers. She advises young Muslim women on how to be Muslim in America. WISE promotes women's rights internationally. Khan, who champions religious freedom and pluralism, was highly critical of Peter King's congressional hearing into the radicalization of American Muslims (2011–12). Her memoir, *Born with Wings*, was published in 2018. The FDNY fire marshal describes his work as his personal response to the Qur'ān's injunction that to save one life is equivalent to saving all of humanity (Q5:32). "To be a good Muslim," he says, "you have to serve people."[23] On 9/11, as he sped toward the towers, he thought, "Oh, in the back of my head, please don't be Muslims doing this. And I just felt ah, I just felt sick."[24] That act of terror clearly contradicts what he believes to be Islam's respect for life, and its humanitarian values. I have experienced similar sentiments when I hear an initial report of an act of terror. I am aware that, if it becomes known that the perpetrators were Muslim, I will find it even harder to challenge the stereotype that all Muslims are prone to commit such acts. There have been times when, were it not for my sense of vocation to engage with Islam and Muslims, I have contemplated turning to a less complex and controversial field. My friendship with so many peace-loving Muslims who strive to create more just societies, however, reminds me that misrepresentation of Islam commits the sin of giving false witness, and must be countered.

Another resource that provides data on what Muslims think, how they view the West and their opinions on a range of issues, results from Gallup Poll's multiyear research project (between 2001 and 2007) when thousands of thousands of Muslims of both sexes, different ages and different socio-economic status in rural and urban settings were asked questions in thirty-five countries. Questions included:

> *Is Islam to blame for terrorism?*
> *Why is there so much anti-Americanism in the Muslim world?*
> *Who are the extremists?*

---

23. *Muhammad: Legacy of a Prophet*, script, 11.
24. *Muhammad: Legacy of a Prophet*, script, 47.

> *Where are the moderates?*
> *What do Muslim women really want?*

The results are presented in a video, *Inside Islam: What a Billion Muslims Really Think* (2009), and in a book, *Who Speaks for Islam* (2007), by John L. Esposito and Dalia Mogahed. Writing in 2013, I commented that "the sample was large enough to produce data on what more than a billion Muslims think and believe." I continued,

> For example, a majority "admire the West's political freedoms" and "value and desire greater self-determination." A "significant majority" in "many countries" does not want religious leaders "defining a country's constitution" while "large percentages . . . think that women's rights should be identical to men's."[25]

Ninety percent of Bangladeshi, 80 percent of Indonesian, and 58 percent of Saudi men think that women should vote.[26] A majority did not think that the United States is serious about promoting democracy and thought that the West denigrates Muslims, although many (58 percent among "radicals") want better relations with the United States despite seeing it as "aggressive," "decadent," and "ruthless."[27] The data challenges many stereotypes and assumptions and is well worth reading. The *Document on Human Fraternity*, signed February 4, 2019, by Pope Francis and the Grand Imam of Al Azhar, calls us to reject "the discriminatory use of the term minorities," raising questions about how the language we use may perpetuate the othering of Muslims as not really welcome by engendering "feelings of isolation and inferiority."

Works of Fiction and Muslim Experience in Post 9/11 America

Post 9/11, Muslims have experienced harassment and intimidation, including routinely being selected for additional security screening when traveling and physical attacks and verbal abuse when simply going about their daily lives, which all makes them feel unwelcome in their own land. They are told to go back to where they came from despite being born in the United States or being naturalized citizens with the same right as any

---

25. Bennett, "New Directions," 281.
26. Esposito and Mogahed, *Billion Muslims*, 51.
27. Bennett, "New Directions," 281.

other US citizen to regard this as their home. People thought to look like Muslims (a dubious concept, given their ethnic diversity), too, experience similar treatment. My son is almost always singled out for enhanced security when entering the United States. According to Pew Research there were 307 reported incidents of anti-Muslim hate crimes in 2016. Soon after 9/11, many Muslim charities and organizations had their assets frozen, accused of receiving funds from or having links with terrorists. In New York, police infiltrated mosques to gather intelligence on potential terror risks. The Council on American Islamic Relations (CAIR) recently reported that anti-Muslim incidents comprised 31 percent of all bias reports dealt with by the FBI between January and March 2018. The FBI had stripped CAIR's of its consultative status in 2009. Forty-three out of the United States' fifty states have debated anti-*Shariʿāh* laws since 2014. Fourteen have been enacted. Technically, *Shariʿāh* refers to a set of guiding principles rather than to a system of laws. These principles require interpretation which, in practice, varies considerably across time and space. This concern with *Shariʿāh* law as somehow a danger to the United States' constitution and legal system was artificially manufactured by anti-Muslim organizations such as the American Freedom Law Center and the ACT for America, which the Southern Poverty Law Center has designated as a hate group.

Among other works, I recommend a novel, *Submission* (2012), by Amy Waldman, and a film, *My Name Is Khan* (2010), directed by Karan Johar, for providing insight into the post 9/11 experience of American Muslims. These could be read or watched in church study groups and discussed. As we attempt to develop empathy with our Muslim neighbors, such works of fiction—rather than statistical reports—provide a more thought-provoking and engaging medium to become better informed on a range of issues surrounding 9/11's impact on American Muslims and on the United States itself. This connects with current debates on immigration generally. Waldman's novel was our "one book" at SUNY New Paltz during November 2012. I had the pleasure of meeting Amy when she came to campus and of participating in a panel discussion of the novel. The setting is a competition to select a design for the 9/11 memorial which takes place two years after the attack. The actual event is never specifically mentioned but this identification is obvious. The jury chose a proposal by Mo Khan for a geometric designed garden. They were unaware of his Muslim background since submissions were anonymous. They learned of this from the media, which had discovered the winner's identity. Very quickly, public outrage that a

Muslim had won the competition broke out, leaving the jury to deal with the consequences. Characters in the novel include relatives of 9/11 victims. One of these is a Bangladeshi widow whose undocumented husband had died in the attack. She is concerned that he may not be recognized by the memorial because he was not a legal resident and that she will be deported before the birth of her child, who would be a US citizen.[28] Donald Trump would like to end birthright citizenship, which coincidentally would reduce the number of Muslim citizens too. The same newspaper that discovered Mo's identity reported her immigration status. She is stabbed to death later in the novel on her way to the airport to return to Bangladesh. The media had "informed the whole world when she would leave."[29] A firefighter opposed to Mo's design pulls off a woman's headscarf.[30] He later apologizes.[31] For a Muslim to design the memorial was a stab "in the heart," which the jury should hear "loud and clear."[32] What would be next, "the Crescent over the Capitol?"[33] Among slurs on Islam we read that it sanctions lying; Mo had concealed his identity.[34] Throughout the novel, Waldman helps us understand how 9/11 affected New York as a city, American Muslims, and the whole of the United States. A *New York Times* reviewer observes that the book echoes the 24/7 coverage that 9/11 generated, and explores how politicians from the right and the left made political capital from 9/11. We read that one journalist commented, "The problem with Islam is Islam"[35] and went out of her way to be sensational and unbalanced in her reporting. The description of attacks on Muslims and mosques reads like actual media coverage; eleven mosque desecrations, a roasted pig and dog feces left outside mosques while "twenty-five Muslim self-defense squads" patrolled in response.[36] The jury try to persuade Mo, who is a nominal rather than religious Muslim, to change or withdraw his submission, which one tabloid calls a "Victory Garden."[37] It would be a "Mohammed Memorial" dedicated

28. Waldman, *Submission*, 71.
29. Waldman, *Submission*, 253.
30. Waldman, *Submission*, 153.
31. Waldman, *Submission*, 183.
32. Waldman, *Submission*, 83.
33. Waldman, *Submission*, 132.
34. Waldman, *Submission*, 132, 245.
35. Waldman, *Submission*, 106.
36. Waldman, *Submission*, 234.
37. Waldman, *Submission*, 127.

to a man who "took slaves, raided caravans and married a six-year old."[38] Mo becomes the target of verbal attack from some imams, too, who accuse him of blasphemy for apparently suggesting that "a man wrote the Quran"[39] during the public hearing about his design. Mo, referring to the Qur'ān's description of paradise, had said, "the Gardens predate Islam . . . maybe man wrote the Quran in response to" the "context: compared to the desert, gardens seemed heavenly."[40] Mo's response to being "analyzed, judged and invented"[41] by strangers when he was "if not an atheist . . . an agnostic, which perhaps made him not a Muslim at all"[42] echoes Salman Rushdie's "it seems bizarre, and wholly inappropriate to be described as some sort of heretic after having lived my life as a secular, pluralist, eclectic man."[43] Others claimed that his design was really paying homage to the terrorists because, they said, it represented the Paradise where they believed they would reside as martyrs after the attack. Responding to the assumption that art produced by a Muslim must therefore be Islamic, Mo described his design as "lines on a plane," adding, "Geometry doesn't belong to a single culture."[44] We also see how Mo becomes self-conscious of how others perceive him: "Customarily brusque on work sites" after 9/11, "he had become gingerly, polite, careful to give no cause for alarm or criticism."[45] At LAX airport, officers interrogate him; where had he been born, what did he do in LA, did he love the United States, how often did he think about *jihād*.[46] Critics wanted to know whether Mo supported the US invasion of Afghanistan. Did he "subscribe to all the conspiracy theories" that 9/11 "was an inside job." Did he think that "America got what it deserved?"[47] Waldman shows us how the event exacerbated existing political, ethnic, religious, and class tensions in the city. There is some overlap between this work and the controversy generated by the so-called Ground Zero mosque project. The site proposed during 2010 for an Islamic Cultural Center was

38. Waldman, *Submission*, 248.
39. Waldman, *Submission*, 239.
40. Waldman, *Submission*, 246.
41. Waldman, *Submission*, 120.
42. Waldman, *Submission*, 28.
43. Rushdie, *Imaginary Homelands*, 405.
44. Waldman, *Submission*, 269.
45. Waldman, *Submission*, 25.
46. Waldman, *Submission*.
47. Waldman, *Submission*, 161.

actually two blocks away from Ground Zero. The center was to be a venue for interfaith exchange. However, opponents saw this as a violation of what they consider to be Ground Zero's sanctity. A *Breitbart* contributor called it "a middle finger to the American people."[48] After a great deal of heated debate involving national as well as local politicians and religious leaders, the sponsors withdrew. Rosemary R. Corbett's *Making Moderate Islam: Sufism, Service, and the "Ground Zero Mosque" Controversy* (2017) based on ten years fieldwork research chronicles the events surrounding the controversy with a great deal of information about reactions to the proposal, how Islam has featured in US foreign policy, the central figure involved in the project, and Muslim responses to 9/11. For some, Ground Zero is sacred space for everyone except Muslims, whose presence or proximity is seen as defiling.

My Name Is Khan (directed by Karan Johar, script by Shibano Bathia) features the Bollywood mega star Shah Ruck Khan, who plays Rizwan Khan. Scenes introduce us to his childhood in his native Kashmir. He is a high-functioning autistic child with an extraordinary ability to fix broken machinery and to use whatever is available to solve technical problems. Scenes include a Muslim-Hindu riot. Rizwan's autism is cleverly used throughout the film to allow him leeway to say exactly what he thinks while also having difficulty expressing his emotions. Scenes switch back and forth along a timeline. In the opening scene, we see Rizwan taken aside in an airport for additional screening and missing his flight to Washington, DC, where he wanted to meet President Bush. This immediately raised the TSA officers' suspicion. Why would a Muslim want to meet the president? Rizwan wanted to tell him that he was called Khan, and was not a terrorist. Later in the film we learn why Rizwan had set out to meet Bush. He had joined his younger brother and his sister-in-law, a psychology professor (who was the first to recognize his autism), in San Francisco after their mother's death, and was working as a salesman for the cosmetic firm where his brother was a senior employee. In a hair salon, where he was selling the cosmetics, he meets Mandira Khan, a beautiful divorced Hindu, and after an amusing romance they marry. Moving to a suburb, where Mandira opens her own salon, they begin a happy middle-class life together with Mandira's son, Sameer, with whom Rizwan had bonded. September 11 shattered this idyllic life, clearly intended to depict the American Dream. Together, the couple watch the Twin Towers collapse in horror, little knowing how this would bring unspeakable tragedy to their lives. At a fund-raising vigil for

---

48. Geller, "It's Official."

the victims of 9/11, Khan astonishes onlookers by donating his *zakāh*, $3,502.50, a considerable sum compared with most of the donations. When Rizwan began reciting the first *sūrah*, dressed in his white robe and wearing his prayer cap, those near him move away, looking at him with alarm. Tragedy soon follows. Their friend, Mark, a journalist, is killed on assignment in Afghanistan. His son, Reese, until then Rizwan's closest friend, begins ignoring him, which starts when he shrugs off his embrace at Mark's funeral. Opening his locker at school, Sameer sees images of Bin Laden posted inside by some of his fellow students. In one scene, Reese yells at him, "You know what you people are nobody's best friends. All you people care is about your damn 'Jihad' or whatever." Customers cancel their bookings at Mandira's salon, which they have to close. In other scenes, we see a Hindu-owned motel's windows smashed because the owner was assumed to be a Muslim. In another, a salesman in an electronic store is harassed simply for being a Muslim. In another, a school teacher tells her class that Islam is the most violent religion because it teaches *jihād*. In another, we learn that a Sikh television reporter had abandoned his turban because Sikhs were being mistaken as Muslims. Rizwan's sister-in-law has her veil ripped off while on campus and is told to leave the country. Then, while again trying to speak with Reese, older youths call Sameer "Osama's son" and "bloody Paki," attack him and leave him mortally injured on the playing field. He is later found, taken to hospital, and dies. Grief stricken, Mandira blames this tragedy on her decision to use Rizwan's name, Khan, and on having married a Muslim, saying that she will leave him. Not fully comprehending what was happening, Rizwan says that as the house belongs to her, he should leave, but when should he return? Mandira says, when you have told the president that your name is Khan, and you are not a terrorist. This is why Rizwan set out in his quest to meet Bush, who he missed several times. Once he paid $500 to attend a church fund-raising event for children in Africa, where Bush was the chief guest, but was turned away because he was not a Christian. Leaving the money, he said use it for Africans who are not Christian. When he eventually manages to stand near enough to Bush, who is visiting a university campus, to shout that he is not a terrorist, bystanders mishear him thinking he had said that he *was a terrorist*. He is arrested, taken to a secure facility and subjected to various techniques—torture in other words—to make him give up information on Al-Qaeda. Earlier, he had informed the FBI about a terrorist sympathizer he met in a mosque. This eventually led to his release. By then, his mission to meet the president had made the headlines, but the young Indian student journalists who had decided to take up his case as their project (puzzled that anyone would shout out that they were a terrorist) still did not know why. One of the most moving scenes in the movie follows next. Earlier, Rizwan had befriended a black family in a fictitious Georgian town. Seeing on the news that the town had been struck by a hurricane, he hurried to help the victims. Once his humanitarian action became known through the two young journalists who were tracking his movements with the help of a hacker, hundreds of Muslims respond by joining him. We see Rizwan repeatedly acting generously toward others, refusing to separate people by race or creed. We hear him recite Q5:32. The film challenges the stereotypes of Muslims hating all non-Muslims (on stereotypes, see also *Struggling with Stereotypes* on the Harvard Pluralism Project website). At the end of the movie, Rizwan, reunited with Mandira, meets president-elect Barack Obama, and is able to tell him that his name is Khan, and he is not a terrorist. Rizwan almost died in one scene when, while still in Georgia, a supporter of the militant he had informed the FBI about stabbed him. Several scenes also show how, after 9/11, some Muslims have felt it necessary to minimize the public display of their faith in order to avoid harassment. After being attacked, Rizwan's sister-in-law stopped wearing her veil when her husband advised her that "these people would not understand" but God would. Later, though, she decided to wear it again with pride, telling her class, "My hijab is not just my religious identity. It is a part of my existence. It's me." A young Muslim couple whom Rizwan meets on his travels advise him, at a refreshment stop, when he began to leave them at prayer time, that he should pray according to place and circumstance. Rizwan's response was that prayer did not depend on place or circumstance or on the people around you but only on your belief. Rizwan prays alone while the Muslim couple look nervously on and bystanders do so with suspicion.

Ideas for Discussion

A church discussion could begin by reading Todd Green's concluding chapter to his book *Presumed Guilty*, "Assuming the Best of Our Muslim Neighbors,"[49] in order to adopt guidelines for relating with Muslims. Todd draws on Krister Stendal's three rules of interfaith understanding to suggest

---

49. Green, *Presumed Guilty*, 163–79.

how Christians can see the best in their Muslim neighbors and work with them toward a juster, more peaceful world.

Discussion could then invite participants to choose scenes or passages that describe specific non-Muslim responses to 9/11 or to the controversy at the center of *Submission*, and think about how they might respond themselves. How might they deal with a situation when someone voices the view that Muslims should go home, for example. How do participants react to the opening scene (at the airport) in the film, to the scene in the secure facility, or to Rizwan's experience at the fund-raising event? Participants could also choose scenes or passages that inform us about Muslim experiences post 9/11 and reflect on whether there are ways that we can offer support to Muslim neighbors in dealing with Islamophobia. How would we feel if we found ourselves being defined by others in ways we do not recognize as Mo did? The Shoulder to Shoulder *Toolkit* says that we should "stand up" for Muslims. How might we do this? Are we aware of ways in which local Muslims face discrimination? How might we show solidarity? Would we consider displaying a banner expressing this outside our church or does this betray persecuted Christians in Muslim majority states? Would we wear a *ḥijāb* as did New Zealand's prime minister Jacindra Arden and other non-Muslim women after the March 15, 2019, massacre of forty-nine Muslims in two Christchurch mosques by a white supremacist as an expression of solidarity? Participants could identify scenes and passages that challenge their own attitudes, and discuss how. Those that represent negative stereotypes could be contrasted with those that challenge these. Would participants have objected to a 9/11 memorial designed by a Muslim; if so, why, and if not, why. Were the criticisms of the "Islamic" elements of Mo's design justified and how do participants respond to his refusal to modify this?

Suggestions for Forming Partnerships for Social Action

The documentary *Different Books, Common Word* (2010), produced by Robert Parham and Cliff Vaughn as a result of the Baptist-Muslim initiative described in chapter 5, is helpful here. The downloadable study guide includes discussion questions beginning with asking how we felt when we first heard of the Oklahoma City bombing in 1995 when many quickly assumed that Muslims were responsible. Citing texts from the Qur'ān and Bible on caring for those in need, the guide asks Baptists whether they are familiar with the former, and Muslims how familiar they are with the latter. How did viewers respond to faces in the opening montage that were very different from their own? How have our upbringings affected the ways in which we view people whose appearance is different from ours? The guide invites people to share if they have experienced a violent act because of their appearance or religion and if they have ever reached out to victims of such an attack, if so, why, and if not, why not.

The first step in contemplating cooperative action with Muslims is to identify partners. Your church may already enjoy contact with a local Mosque either because of personal relationships or through membership of an interfaith council. You may decide that working through such a council on adopting a project is the best way forward rather than attempting to do this as an individual church. The documentary usefully features a number of initiatives including how Baptists and Muslims combined resources in Texas to assist hurricane victims.

Building on the Baptist-Muslim initiative's invitation for shared study of our two scriptures, I recommend forming study groups, perhaps drawing on the scriptural reasoning model, as an important step in articulating a common spiritual vision for a partnership in social involvement. What are our scriptural mandates for the type of projects we might contemplate, such as running a food bank, a warming shelter, or a free health clinic? What are the values we share that motivate us to seek for justice, peace and the common good and what do we mean by these high-sounding words? My congregation ran the county warming shelter for several years but this year could not do so due to refurbishment plans. Initially, we tried to identify a replacement venue. Then members of the interfaith council expressed interest. Through this, a new location was found and the council is coordinating volunteers. For the last two years, our local synagogue has hosted the free Christmas meal.

An important question, once a project is identified, is how might we each bear witness to our faiths through such a project? Some critics of the "social gospel" argue that there is no real distinction between churches providing community services and a secular not-for-profit doing so. My response is that our motives differ. Services are offered without any expectation of a quid pro quo in terms of clients embracing our faiths but this does not mean that we are silent about why we do what we do, which for me is the God-mandated task of loving our neighbors in practical ways. Scriptural reasoning, thus far, has attracted mainly academic participants although it is not a faith-neutral practice but one that is profoundly concerned with discovering truths about God and humanity. Those involved commit to listening with respect to all contributions. There is no obligation for everyone to recognize that other scriptures have any authority but everyone is expected to acknowledge that they do have authority for those who see these as God's word. Scriptural reasoning (SR) allows those for whom the passage studied is sacred to give the first opinion on meaning while recognizing that this is not the final word. David Ford, on whose chapter the above paragraph draws, says that consensus or agreement is not the aim; participants may conclude by acknowledging, and respecting, deep differences. However, as practiced, scriptural reasoning seeks to prioritize meanings that promote "the fulfilment of God's purposes of peace."[50] While SR involves Jews, Christians, and Muslims there is no good reason why it cannot be adapted for the specific context of Christians and Muslims scrutinizing their sacred scriptures to identify content and meaning that can inform shared action. Of course, a tripartite project is certainly an option. Ford, who invited me to teach at the Cambridge Interfaith Programme's first summer school, says that SR offers a third choice after "assimilation" and "confrontation" when religions meet. This is the option of "mutually critical engagement . . . aimed at transforming the public sphere for the common good." Participants in SR should delve deeper into their own scriptures, deeper into "wisdom seeking conversations with each other, and with all who have a stake in the common good."[51] Private reasoning and wisdom sharing will become shared wisdom for public debate and action as a resource for peacemaking and human development.

Conclusion: Some Additional Suggestions

Where Christians and Muslims engage in common study and in shared action, there is evidence that negative stereotypes yield to more nuanced understandings. This is especially true when theological exchange such as through scriptural reasoning or other ways of engaging with each other's scripture results in common action, whether running a food pantry or joint humanitarian response to a natural disaster. Many Christians realize that while some self-defined Muslims do act violently, and may even hate the United States, most—if not all—of their Muslim neighbors do not. These

---

50. Ford, "Interfaith Wisdom," 5.
51. Ford, "Interfaith Wisdom," 20.

neighbors share many of our aspirations and values, which can meaningfully be identified in dialogue and scriptural sharing. Some Christians go further; while disagreeing with how a minority of Muslims (if indeed they are Muslim) act out their hostility toward the United States, they reflect self-critically on how US foreign policy, economic and political power might negatively impact others' lives, other states and regions of the world. Perhaps one way of expressing solidarity with Muslims on these issues, when we share their view, is to write to our congressional representatives to express our opinions. Sadly, because millions of Christians still do not meet Muslims and vice versa, Christian ideas about Islam and Muslim ideas about Christianity are still primarily formed by media stereotypes, caricatures, and unchallenged assumptions. However, even meeting does not automatically result in viewing one another more cordially unless we are each open to listening and learning, and to revising our ideas. Those of us who are Christian need to ignore the mass media and look instead to the type of resources, including those produced or broadcast by PBS, described in this chapter. Scriptural study as described above should be embedded in as many local programs as possible inside and outside the academy. Ideally, this will become part of how Christians and Muslims nurture their children's faith, perhaps using jointly written resources. Perhaps this should be taken further. Might not Christian clergy, rabbis, and imams be formed for ministry in shared institutions; Hartford Seminary may represent a model here. In some respects, 9/11 presents a challenge to those who champion interfaith harmony, suggesting that it is wishful thinking or pie in the sky. On the other hand, some Christians and Muslims refuse to allow the heinous acts of a few to compromise their commitment to forge improved, better-informed, more astutely constructed interfaith relations. Christians involved in the formal dialogues described in my previous chapter are somewhat out of step with the majority of Americans, for whom Islam is problematic. As America becomes more pluralist, with the current white majority of European extraction predicted to be a minority by 2060,[52] challenging stereotypes, acting together on translating shared values into practice as championed by this chapter, to make society safer, more equitable and just for all despite setbacks is a goal worth struggling to achieve.

---

52. US Census Bureau, "New Census Bureau Report."

Conclusion

Although much of this book shares my grappling with theological issues on the Christian-Muslim agenda—the dialogue of theological exchange—I have become convinced that the dialogues of life and of action are more vital. As we respond to social challenges together, we may see our common humanity more clearly. In the process of meeting, planning, and acting, I believe that we will find ourselves sharing at the deeper level of spiritual exchange. Ultimately, resolution of or rapprochement on the many theological issues that apparently divide us may only be resolved when we account before God for our actions on behalf of our neighbors in need, or admit that we lived too selfishly. I have long contemplated the advice of Q5:38 and of Q2:148, speaking to the peoples of the book (Muslims, Jews, and Christians). Q5:38 says,

> And We have revealed to you, [O Muḥammad], the Book in truth, confirming that which preceded it of the Scripture and as a criterion over it. So judge between them by what Allah has revealed and do not follow their inclinations away from what has come to you of the truth. To each of you We prescribed a law and a method. Had Allah willed, He would have made you one nation [united in religion], but [He intended] to test you in what He has given you; so race to [all that is] good. To Allah is your return all together, and He will [then] inform you concerning that over which you used to differ.

Q2:148 says,

> And each one has a goal toward which he turns so vie with one another in good works. Wheresoever you may be, Allah will bring you all together. Lo! Allah is Able to do all things.

As a minimum, if common action is for us a step too far, we should at least ensure that what we say about Muslims passes the litmus test of fair witness. If Muslims hear us speak ignorantly and falsely about Islam they are unlikely to listen to anything we say about our own faith, which means

CONCLUSION

that truthfulness is to be commended as a better missionary strategy in any effort to win Muslims for Christ, which many regard as the primary Christian task in our relations with Muslims. I have, though, stated from the outset my conviction that salvation is the gift and work of the Holy Spirit; our calling is to share our beliefs sensitively and respectfully while leaving results to the Spirit of the Living God. Some call Jesus "Lord, Lord" but do not do what he says (Luke 6:46). Others, perhaps, do not say the words but live lives that mirror Jesus' generosity, compassion, and humanness. Some see these as his "other sheep"(John 10:16). Striving together in loving and compassionate service of others, I believe, pleases God more than engaging in repetitive theological debate. This can divert us from more vital and urgent tasks in our communities, in our nations, and in the world itself. Talking about love, justice, and peace can clarify and deepen our understanding of these but practicing love-in-action and championing peace with justice for all is the vital task which God calls us to undertake in God's name. I hope that the more practical suggestions for Christian-Muslim engagement set out in chapter 6, drawing on forty years of experience, will help some readers to develop partnerships with Muslim neighbors in their communities and beyond.

Bibliography

A Common Word between Us and You. 5 year anniversary ed. Amman: Royal Hashemite House, 2012. Available at https://www.acommonword.com/a-common-word-between-us-and-you-5-year-anniversary-edition/.
Ali, Monica. *Brick Lane: A Novel.* New York: Scribner, 2003.
———. *Brick Lane.* Film. Directed by Sarah Gavron. London: Film4, 2008.
'Alī, Syed Amīr. *The Spirit of Islam; or, The Life and Teachings of Mohammed.* Calcutta: Lahiri, 1902.
Amman Foundation. *The Amman Interfaith Message.* Jordan, 2007. Available at http://ammanmessage.com/the-amman-interfaith-message/.
———. *The Amman Message.* Jordan, 2004. Available at http://ammanmessage.com/the-amman-message-full/.
Andrae, Tor. *Muḥammad: The Man and His Faith.* London: Allen and Unwin, 1936.
Askari, Hasan. *Alone to Alone.* Pudsey, UK: Seven Mirrors, 1991.
———. "The Real Presence of Jesus in Islam." In *Jesus in the World's Faiths: Leading Thinkers from Five Religions Reflect on His Meaning*, edited by Gregory A. Barker, 142–46. Maryknoll: Orbis, 2005.
———. *Spiritual Quest: An Interreligious Perspective.* Pudsey, UK: Seven Mirrors, 1991.
Aydin, Mehmet. *Modern Western Christian Theological Understandings of Muslims since the Second Vatican Council.* Washington, DC: Council for Research in Values and Philosophy, 2002.
Bar Hebraeus, Gregory. *The Chronography.* Translated by E. A. Wallis Budge. 2 vols. Oxford: Oxford University Press, 1932.
Benedict XVI. *Regensburg-Lecture.* 2006. Available at http://www.catholic-ew.org.uk/Home/News/2006/2006-Offline/Full-Text-of-the-Pope-Benedict-XVI-s-Regensburg-Lecture.
Bennett, Clinton. "Christian-Muslim Relations in the USA: A Postmodern Analysis after 9/11." In *Contemporary Muslim-Christian Encounters: Developments, Diversity and Dialogue*, edited by Paul Hedges, 151–66. London: Bloomsbury, 2015.
———. "A Christian Response to the Absence of the Cross in Islam." In Singh, *Jesus and the Cross*, 171–79.
———. "Christian Trinity and Muslim Attributes: An Invitation to Spiritual Exploration." *Bulletin of the Henry Martyn Institute of Islamic Studies* 10 (1991) 38–42. Republished in *Approaches, Foundations, Issues, and Models of Interfaith Relations*, edited by David Emmanuel Singh and Robert Schick, 265–70. Delhi: Indian Society for Promoting Christian Knowledge and Henry Martin Institute of Islamic Studies, Hyderabad, 2001.
———. "Christians and Muḥammad." In *Routledge Handbook on Christian-Muslim Relations*, edited by David Thomas, 296–303. London: Routledge, 2017.

BIBLIOGRAPHY

———. "Day the Baptists Met the Muslims." *Baptist Times*, May 16, 1985.

———. "Dialogue: Witness or Treason?" *Current Dialogue* (World Council of Churches) June 14, 1988, 32–35, 44; also in *Inter-religious Dialogue: A Paradox?*, edited by the Silsilah editorial board, 172–79. Zamboanga City, Philippines: Silsilah, 1991.

———. "Flirtation with Unitarianism." *Inquirer*, March 7, 1981.

———, ed. "Focus on the Salman Rushdie Affair." Special issue, *Discernment: An Ecumenical Journal of Inter-Religious Encounter* 4.2 (1990).

———. "Henry Stubbe." In *Christian-Muslim Relations: A Bibliographical History*, edited by David Thomas and John Chesworth, 8:472–84. Leiden: Brill, 2016.

———. "Thomas Helwys." In *Christian-Muslim Relations: A Bibliographical History*, edited by David Thomas and John Chesworth, 8: 148-151. Leiden: Brill, 2016.

———. *In Search of Jesus: Insider-Outsider Images*. London: Continuum, 2001.

———. *In Search of Muḥammad*. London: Cassell, 1998.

———. *In Search of the Sacred: Anthropology and the Study of Religion*. London: Cassel, 1996.

———. *Interpreting the Qur'an: A Guide for the Uninitiated*. London: Continuum, 2010.

———. *Muslims and Modernity: An Introduction to the Issues and Debates*. London: Continuum, 2005.

———. "New Directions: The Who, Why, What, How and Where of Islamic Studies." In *The Bloomsbury Companion to Islamic Studies*, edited by Clinton Bennett, 259–83. London: Bloomsbury, 2013.

———. "US Military." In *Encyclopedia of American Muslim History*, edited by Edward E. Curtis IV, 561-564. NY: Facts on File, 2010

———. "Resurrection as Lived Praxis: Reflecting on Christian and Muslim Ideas about the 'Resurrection.'" In *Jesus and the Resurrection: Reflections of Christians from Islamic Contexts*, edited by David Emmanuel Singh, 155–62. Oxford: Regnum, 2013.

———. "Saints, Incarnation and Christian-Muslim Relations: Reflections Inspired by Encountering Bangladeshi Islam." In *Jesus and the Incarnation: Reflections of Christians from Islamic Contexts*, edited by David Emmanuel Singh, 99–111. Oxford: Regnum, 2011.

———. "The Salman Rushdie Affair: Some Underlying Issues." *Discernment: An Ecumenical Journal of Inter-Religious Encounter* 4.2 (1990) 3–11.

———. "A Theological Appreciation of Lewis Bevan Jones (1880–1960): Baptist Pioneer in Christian-Muslim Relations." *Baptist Quarterly* 32 (1988) 237–52.

———. *Understanding Christian-Muslim Relations Past and Present*. New York: Continuum, 2008.

———. *Victorian Images of Islam*. London: Grey Seal, 1992; Piscataway, NJ: Gorgias, 2009, 2014.

Bennett, Clinton, and Sarwar Alam, eds. *Sufism, Pluralism and Democracy*. Sheffield, UK: Equinox, 2017.

Bennett, Clinton, and Charles M. Ramsey, eds. *South Asian Sufis: Devotion, Deviation, and Destiny*. London: Continuum, 2012.

Bennett, Clinton, et al. *Researching into Teaching Methods in Colleges and Universities*. London: Kogan Page, 1996; Abingdon: Routledge, 2013.

Berjak, Raif. "Suffism." In *The Qur'an: An Encyclopedia*, edited by Oliver Leaman, 276–77. London: Routledge, 2006.

Beydoon, Khaled A. *American Islamophobia: Understanding the Roots and Rise of Fear*. Oakland: University of California Press, 2019.

Borrmans, Maurice. *Guidelines for Dialogue between Christians and Muslims*. New York: Paulist, 1990.
British Council of Churches. *Relations with People of Other Faiths: Guidelines on Dialogue in Britain*. London: British Council of Churches, 1983.
Brown, Stuart E. *Meeting in Faith: Twenty Years of Christian-Muslim Conversations Sponsored by the World Council of Churches*. Geneva: WCC Publication, 1989.
Calvin, John. *Institutes of the Christian Religion*. Edited by Anthony Uyl. Translated by H. Beveridge. Ingersoll, Ontario: Devoted, 2016.
Camacho, Daniel José. "Why Mark Anthony Conditt—a White Christian—Isn't Called a Terrorist." *Guardian*, March 23, 2018. https://www.theguardian.com/commentisfree/2018/mar/23/mark-anthony-conditt-terrorism-christianity.
Caner, Ergun Mehmut, and Emir Fethi Caner. *Unveiling Islam: An Insider's Look at Muslim Life and Belief*. Grand Rapids: Kregel, 2002.
Council of Churches for Britain and Ireland. *In Good Faith: The Four Principles of Interfaith Dialogue : A Brief Guide for the Churches*. London: CCBI Inter-Church House, 1991.
Cragg, Kenneth R. *The Call of the Minaret*. New York: Oxford University Press, 1956; Maryknoll: Orbis, 1985; Oxford: Oneworld, 2000.
———. "The Cross and Power: The Parting of the Ways." In Singh, *Jesus and the Cross*, 33–46.
———. Introduction to *City of Wrong: A Friday in Jerusalem*, by M. Kamel Hussein, translated by Kenneth Cragg, 9–26. Oxford: Oneworld, 1994.
———. *Muḥammad and the Christian: A Question of Response*. London: Darton, Longman and Todd, 1984.
———. *The Pen and the Faith: Eight Modern Muslim Writers and the Qur'an*. London: Allen and Unwin, 1985.
———. "The Qur'an and the Cross: Less Absence than You Think." In Singh, *Jesus and the Cross*, 177–86.
Daniel, Norman. *Islam and the West: The Making of an Image*. Oxford: Oneworld, 1997.
Deedat, Ahmed. *Crucifixion or Cruci-fiction*. Durban: Islamic Propagation Centre International, 1984.
Dey, Amit. *Ṣūfism in India*. Calcutta: Ratna Prakashan, 1996.
Document on Human Fraternity for World Peace and Living Together. Rome: Vatican, 2019. Available at http://w2.vatican.va/content/francesco/en/travels/2019/outside/documents/papa-francesco_20190204_documento-fratellanza-umana.html.
Eaton, Richard M. *The Rise of Islam and the Bengal Frontier, 1204–1760*. Berkeley: University of California Press, 1993.
Esack, Farid. *The Qur'an: A User's Guide*. Oxford: Oneworld, 2005.
———. *Qur'an, Liberation & Pluralism: An Islamic Perspective of Interreligious Solidarity against Oppression*. Oxford: Oneworld, 1997.
Esposito, John L. "Islam and the West: Beyond the Green Menace." *Current History: A Journal of Contemporary World Affairs* 579 (1994) 19–24.
Esposito, John L., and Dalia Mogahed. *Who Speaks for Islam? What a Billion Muslims Really Think*. Washington, DC: Gallup, 2008.
Esposito, John L., et al. *Asian Islam in the 21st Century*. Oxford: Oxford University Press, 2008.
Fisk, Samuel. *Election and Predestination: Keys to a Clearer Understanding*. Eugene, OR: Wipf and Stock, 2000.

BIBLIOGRAPHY

Ford, David F. "An Interfaith Wisdom: Scriptural Reasoning between Jews, Christians and Muslims." In *The Promise of Scriptural Reasoning*, edited by David F. Ford and C. C. Pecknold, 1–23. Oxford: Blackwell, 2006.

Gairdner, William Temple. *The Rebuke of Islam*. London: United Council for Missionary Education, 1920.

Gavron, Sarah, et al. *Brick Lane*. [Wevelge]: BrunBro Home Entertainment, 2010.

Geller, Pamela. "It's Official: Ground Zero Mosque Defeated." *Breitbart*, September 26, 2015. https://www.breitbart.com/politics/2015/09/26/its-official-ground-zero-mosque-defeated/.

Gibbon, Edward. *The History of the Decline and Fall of the Roman Empire*. Vol. 5. London, 1777.

Goodwin, Stephen R. Introduction to *World Christianity in Local Context: Essays in Memory of David A. Kerr*, 1:xii–xxi. London: Continuum, 2011.

Green, Todd H. *Presumed Guilty: Why We Shouldn't Ask Muslims to Condemn Terrorism*. Minneapolis: Fortress, 2018.

Grogan, Ellinor Flora Bosworth Smith. *Reginald Bosworth Smith: A Memoir*. London: Nisbet, 1909.

Hick, John. *God and the Universe of Faiths*. London: Macmillan, 1973; Oxford: Oneworld, 1993.

Hitchens, Christopher. *The Trial of Henry Kissinger*. London: Verso, 2001.

Hogg, Alfred George. "The Christian Attitude to Non-Christian Faith." In *The Authority of the Faith*, edited by the International Missionary Council, 102–25. London: International Missionary Council and Oxford University Press, 1939.

Huntington, Samuel P. "The Clash of Civilizations?" *Foreign Affairs* 72 (1993) 22–49.

———. *The Clash of Civilizations and the Remaking of World Order*. New York: Simon & Schuster, 1996.

Hussein, M. Kamel, and Kenneth R. Cragg. *City of Wrong: A Friday in Jerusalem*. Oxford: Oneworld, 1994.

Ibn Isḥāq, and Guillaume, Alfred. *The Life of Muhammad*. Oxford, 1955.

Ibn Taymīyya, and Tom Michel. *A Muslim Theologian's Response to Christianity: Ibn Taymiyya's Al-Jawab Al-Sahih*. New York: Caravan, 1984.

Iqbal, Muhammad, and M. Saeed Sheikh. *The Reconstruction of Religious Thought in Islam*. Stanford, CA: Stanford University Press, 2012.

Johar, Karim, dir. *My Name Is Khan*. Film. Los Angeles: Twentieth Century Fox Home Entertainment, 2012. Script available at https://www.springfieldspringfield.co.uk/movie_script.php?movie=my-name-is-khan.

Jones, Lewis. *Christianity Explained to Muslims*. Calcutta: YMCA, 1938.

———. *Christ's Ambassador to the Muslims*. London: Fellowship of Faith for Muslims, 1952.

———. *The People of the Mosque: An Introduction to the Study of Islam with Special Reference to India*. London: SCM, 1932; Calcutta, YMCA, 1939.

Johnson, Elizabeth A. *Creation and the Cross: The Mercy of God for a Planet in Peril*. Maryknoll: Orbis, 2019.

Kabbani, Rana. *Letter to Christendom*. London: Time Warner, 1989.

Kanjamala, Augustin, and Siga Arles. *The Future of Christian Mission in India: Toward a New Paradigm for the Third Millennium*. Eugene, OR: Pickwick, 2004.

Karamustafa, Ahmet T. "Ṣūfism." In *The Encyclopedia of Christianity*, edited by Erwin Fahlbusch and Geoffrey William Bromiley, 221–24. Grand Rapids: Eerdmans, 1999.

BIBLIOGRAPHY

Kalylor, Brian. "American Muslim, Baptist Leaders Hold Groundbreaking Meeting." EthicsDaily.com. January 12, 2009. https://ethicsdaily.com/american-muslim-baptist-leaders-hold-groundbreaking-meeting-cms-13745.

Kerr, David A. "Muhammad: Prophet of Liberation; A Christian Perspective from Political Theology." *Studies in World Christianity* 6 (2000) 139–74.

———. "The Prophet Muhammad in Christian Theological Perspective." *International Bulletin of Missionary Research* 8 (1984) 112–16.

Khodr, George. "The Economy of the Spirit." In *Mission Trends: Faith Meets Faith No. 5*, edited by Gerald H. Anderson and Thomas F. Stransky, 36–49. Grand Rapids: Eerdmans, 1981.

Kishi, Katayoun. "Assaults against Muslims in U.S. Surpass 2001 Level." Pew Research Center. November 15, 2017. https://www.pewresearch.org/fact-tank/2017/11/15/assaults-against-muslims-in-u-s-surpass-2001-level/.

Knapp, Arthur Bernard. *The History and Culture of Ancient Western Asia and Egypt.* Chicago: Dorsey, 1988.

Knysh, Alexander D. *Ibn 'Arabi in the Later Islamic Tradition: The Making of a Polemical Image in Medieval Islam.* SUNY Series in Islam. Albany: State University of New York Press, 1999.

Kronemer, Alexander, and Michael Wolfe, producers. *Inside Islam: What a Billion Muslims Really Think.* DVD. Potomac Falls, VA: Unity Productions Foundation, 2010.

———. *Muhammad: Legacy of a Prophet.* DVD. Potomac Falls, VA: Unity Productions Foundation, 2002. Script available at https://www-tc.pbs.org/muhammad/transcripts/muhammad_script.pdf.

Küng, Hans. *Christianity and the World Religions: Paths of Dialogue with Islam, Hinduism and Buddhism.* Maryknoll: Orbis, 1986.

Latourette, Kenneth Scott. *A History of the Expansion of Christianity.* Grand Rapids: Zondervan, 1978.

Lewis, Bernard. "The Roots of Muslim Rage." *Atlantic Monthly*, September 1999, 47–60.

Lewis, Richard D. *When Cultures Collide: Leading across Cultures.* Rev. ed. Boston: Brealey, 2005.

Marshall, David. "Christianity in the Quran." In *Islamic Interpretations of Christianity*, edited by Lloyd Ridgeon, 3–29. Abingdon: Routledge, 2001.

Matar, Nabil. *Henry Stubbe and the Beginnings of Islam.* New York: Columbia University Press, 2014.

Mingana, Alphonse. *The Apology of Timothy the Patriarch before the Caliph Mahdi.* Woodbrooke Studies 2. Cambridge: Heffer, 1928.

Moses, Paul. *The Saint and the Sultan: The Crusades, Islam, and Francis of Assisi's Mission of Peace.* New York: Doubleday Religion, 2009.

Muir, William. *The Apology of al-Kindy.* London: SPCK, 1881.

———. *The Life of Mahomet.* 4 vols. London: Smith and Elder, 1858–1860.

Newbigin, James Edward Lesslie. *The Gospel in a Pluralist Society.* Grand Rapids: Eerdmans, 1989.

Nicholson, Reynold A. *The Mystics of Islam.* London: Routledge, 1914.

Nickel, Gordon. *Narratives of Tampering in the Earliest Commentaries on the Qurʾān.* Leiden: Brill, 2010.

Oborne, Peter. "Do Not Weep for Bernard Lewis, High Priest of War in the Middle East." *Middle East Eye*, May 21, 2018. https://www.middleeasteye.net/opinion/do-not-weep-bernard-lewis-high-priest-war-middle-east.

Ockley, Simon. *The History of the Saracens.* . . . 6th ed. London, 1857.
Padwick, Constance E. *Muslim Devotions.* London: SPCK, 1961.
Pagels, Elaine. *Beyond Belief: The Secret Gospel of Thomas.* New York: Random House, 2003.
Parham, Robert, and Cliff Vaughn. *Different Books, Common Word: Baptists and Muslims.* Nashville: EthicsDaily.com, 2010.
Parrinder, Geoffrey. *Jesus in the Quran.* London: Faber & Faber, 1965; Oxford: Sheldon, 1977; Oneworld, 2003.
Parshall, Phil. *Beyond the Mosque: Christians within Muslim Community.* Grand Rapids: Baker, 1985.
———. "Danger! New Directions in Contextualization." *Evangelical Missions Quarterly* 34 (1998) 404–10.
———. "Going Too Far?" In *Perspectives on the World Christian Movement: Reader*, edited by Ralph D. Winter et al., 663–67. Pasadena, CA: William Carey Library, 1999.
———. *Understanding Muslim Teachings and Traditions: A Guide for Christians.* Grand Rapids: Baker, 2002.
Peters, F. E. *A Reader on Classical Islam.* Princeton: Princeton University Press, 1994.
Pew Research Center. "U.S. Muslims Concerned about Their Place in Society, but Continue to Believe in the American Dream." Pew Research Center. July 26, 2017. https://www.pewforum.org/2017/07/26/findings-from-pew-research-centers-2017-survey-of-us-muslims/.
Pontifical Council for Interreligious Relations. *Dialogue and Proclamation.* Rome: PCIR, 1991. Available at http://www.vatican.va/roman_curia/pontifical_councils/interelg/documents/rc_pc_interelg_doc_19051991_dialogue-and-proclamatio_en.html.
Pope Paul VI. *Nostra Aetate: The Declaration on the Relations of the Church to Non-Christian Religions.* Rome, 1965. Available at http://www.vatican.va/archive/hist_councils/ii_vatican_council/documents/vat-ii_decl_19651028_nostra-aetate_en.html.
Race, Alan. *Christians and Religious Pluralism: Patterns in the Christian Theology of Religions.* London: SCM, 1983.
Rahner, Karl. "Christianity and the Non-Christian Religions." In *Theological Investigations*, 5:115–31. New York: Seabury, 1966.
Ramsey, Charles. *God's Word, Spoken and Otherwise: Sayyid Ahmad Khan (1817–1898); Revelation and Coherence.* History of Christian-Muslim Relations. Leiden: Brill, forthcoming.
Roy, Asim. *The Islamic Syncretistic Tradition in Bengal.* Princeton: Princeton University Press, 1982.
Runnymede Trust, and Gordon Conway. *Islamophobia: A Challenge for Us All.* London: Runnymede Trust, 1997.
Rushdie, Salman. *Imaginary Homelands: Essays and Criticism, 1981–1991.* London: Granta, 1991.
———. *The Satanic Verses.* New York: Viking, 1988.
El Saadawi, Nawal. *The Nawal El Saadawi Reader.* London: Zed, 1997.
Sahas, Daniel J. *John of Damascus on Islam.* Leiden: Brill, 1972.
Said, Edward. *Covering Islam: How the Media and the Experts Determine How We See the Rest of the World.* New York: Vintage, 1997.
———. *Orientalism.* New York: Pantheon, 1978.

BIBLIOGRAPHY

Samir, Samir. K. "The Prophet Muḥammad as Seen by Timothy II and Some Other Arab Christian Authors." In *Syrian Christians under Islam: The First Thousand Years*, edited by D. Thomas, 75–106. Leiden: Brill, 2001.

Sarder, Ziauddin. *Desperately Seeking Paradise: Journeys of a Skeptical Muslim*. London: Granta, 2012.

Sarwar, Muhammad Shaykh, and Brandon Toropov. *The Complete Idiot's Guide to the Koran*. New York: Random House, 2003.

Shoulder to Shoulder Campaign. *Toolkit for Mobilizing to Protect and Support American Muslims*. An evolving resource. https://medium.com/@S2SCampaign/toolkit-for-mobilizing-to-protect-and-support-american-muslims-7901c8bd7aab.

Siddiqui, Ataullah. *Christian-Muslim Dialogue in the Twentieth Century*. London: Palgrave Macmillan, 1997.

Singh, David Emmanuel, ed. *Jesus and the Cross: Reflections of Christians from Islamic Contexts*. Oxford: Regnum, 2008.

Smith, Margaret. *Muslim Women Mystics: The Life and Work of Rábi'a and Other Women Mystics in Islam*. Great Islamic Thinkers. Oxford: Oneworld, 2001.

Smith, Reginald Bosworth. *Mohammed and Mahammedenism*. London, 1876.

Smith, Wilfred Cantwell. "Comparative Religion: Whither and Why?" In *The History of Religions: Essays on Methodology*, edited by M. Eliade and J. Kitagawa, 31–58. Chicago: University of Chicago Press, 1959.

———. *The Meaning and End of Religion: A New Approach to the Religious Traditions of Mankind*. New York: New American Library, 1965.

———. *Towards a World Theology*. London: Macmillan, 1981.

Soueif, Ahdal. *The Map of Love: A Novel*. London: Anchor, 1993.

Spencer, Robert. *Not Peace but a Sword: The Great Chasm between Christianity and Islam*. San Diego: Catholic Answers, 2013.

———. *The Truth about Muhammad: Founder of the World's Most Intolerant Religion*. Washington, DC: Regnery, 2006.

Sprenger, Aloys. *The Life of Mohammed, from Original Sources*. Allahabad: Presbyterian Mission, 1851.

———. *Das Leben und die Lehre des Moḥammad: nach bisher Grösstentheils unbenutzten Quelle*, 4 volumes. Berlin: Nicolaische Verlagsbuchhandlung, 1861.

Stubbe, Henry, and Mahmud Khan Shairani. *An Account of the Rise and Progress of Mahometanism: With the Life of Mahomet and a Vindication of Him and His Religion from the Calumnies of the Christians*. London: Luzac, 1911.

Thomas, David. "Paul of Antioch." In *Christian-Muslim Relations: A Bibliographical History*, edited by David Thomas and Alexander Mallet, 4:8–82. Leiden: Brill, 2012.

Tisdall, William St. Clair. *Christianity and Other Faiths*. London: Scott, 1912.

———. *The Original Sources of the Qur'an*. London: SPCK, 1905.

———. *The Religion of the Crescent*. London: SPCK, 1916.

Travis, John. "The C1 to C6 Spectrum: A Practical Tool for Defining Six Types of 'Christ-Centered Communities' ('C') Found in the Muslim Context." *Evangelical Missions Quarterly* 33 (1998) 407–8.

Uddin, Ṣūfia M. *Constructing Bangladesh: Religion, Ethnicity, and Language in an Islamic Nation*. Islamic Civilization & Muslim Networks. Chapel Hill: University of North Carolina Press, 2006.

US Census Bureau. "New Census Bureau Report Analyzes US Population Projections." March 3, 2015. https://www.census.gov/newsroom/press-releases/2015/cb15-tps16.html.

US Department of State. *American Muslims*. Washington, DC. https://photos.state.gov/libraries/amgov/30145/publications-english/American_Muslims.pdf.

———. *Being Muslim in America*. Washington, DC. https://photos.state.gov/libraries/korea/49271/dwoa_122709/being-muslim-in-america.pdf accessed.

Waldman, Amy. *The Submission: A Novel*. New York: Farrar, Straus and Giroux, 2011.

Wolf, Kenneth B. "A Christian Account of the Life of Muḥammad." In *Medieval Iberia: Readings from Christian, Muslim, and Jewish Sources*, edited by Olivia R. Constable, 48–50. Philadelphia: University of Pennsylvania Press, 1997.

World Council of Churches. *Issues in Christian-Muslim Relations: Ecumenical Considerations*. Geneva: WCC Publications, 1992. Available at https://www.oikoumene.org/en/resources/documents/wcc-programmes/interreligious-dialogue-and-cooperation/interreligious-trust-and-respect/issues-in-christian-muslim-relations-ecumenical-considerations.

World Council of Churches, Pontifical Council for Interreligious Dialogue, and World Evangelical Alliance. *Christian Witness in a Multireligious World: Recommendation for Conduct*. 2011. Available at https://www.oikoumene.org/en/resources/documents/wcc-programmes/interreligious-dialogue-and-cooperation/christian-identity-in-pluralistic-societies/christian-witness-in-a-multi-religious-world.

Zaehner, Robert Charles. *At Sundry Times: An Essay in the Comparison of Religions*. London: Faber & Faber, 1958.

Zwemer, Samuel Marinus. *The Cross above the Crescent*. Grand Rapids: Zondervan, 1941.

———. *The Glory of the Cross*. London: Oliphant, 1928.

———. *The Moslem Christ: An Essay on the Life, Character and Teachings of Jesus*. Edinburgh: Oliphant, Anderson & Ferrier, 1912.

———. *A Moslem Seeker after God: Showing Islam at Its Best in the Life and Teaching of Al-Ghazālī, Mystic and Theologian of the Eleventh Century*. New York: Revell, 1920.

General Index

A Common Word, 77–80
Abraham, 4, 49, 77
Adhikari, Michael Sushil, xxiv
Afghanistan, 86, 87, 93, 98, 100
Ahmadiyya, 66
ʿĀʾisha, 8
Ali, Monica, xxix
Ali, Muhammad, xxviii
Alī, Sayyid Amir, 17
Alliance of Baptists, xxxix, 76, 79
American Baptist Churches USA, 79–80
American Freedom Law Center, 96
American Muslims, 91–93
American Muslim Council, 75
Amman Interfaith Message, 78
Amman Message, 78
Anderson, Leith, 78
Andover Newton Theological School, 79
Andrae, Bishop Tor, 14–15, 22
Anselm of Canterbury, xiv, 68–70
Arden, Jacindra, 102
Arinze, Cardinal Francis, xxvii
Askari, Syed Hasan, xvii, xviii, xx, 23, 65, 72, 74
Aston University, Birmingham, UK, xxvii
Australia, xv, xvi, xvii, xxi
Aydin, Mehmet, 19, 21, 54
Al-Azhar, Cairo, Grand Imam of, 81, 95

Badawi, Imam Zaki, xxix, 90
Bangladesh, xiii, xiv, xvi, xvii, xviii, xix, xx, xxi–xxv, xxvi, xxviii, xxix, xxxviii, 11–12, 26–31, 36, 49, 51, 84, 86, 87, 91, 95, 97
Bangladesh Baptist Church Sangha, xxii, xxiv

Baptist Missionary Society/BMS World Mission, xiv, xv, xvi, xviii, xxiii, xxiv, xx, xxi, xxii, xxiii
Baptist Seminary of the West, 79
Baptist Union of Great Britain, xxvii, xxxiii, xxxviii, xxxix
Baptist World Alliance, 79–80
Baptist-Muslim Dialogue USA, 79
baqāʾ 33–34
barakah, 33
Barisal, xxi, xxiv,
Bathia, Shibano, 99
Baylor University, TX, xxxviii, 57
Being Muslim in America, 93
Benedict XVI, Pope, 78
Beydoun, Khaled A., 86
Bible, xviii, xxiv, xxxiv, 6, 12, 15, 18, 19, 35, 45, 46, 47, 50,-59, 102
Bin Laden, Osama, 87, 100
Birmingham Central Mosque, xxvi, xxvii
Birmingham Community Relations Council, xxvii, xxviii
Birmingham Council of Christian Churches, xxvi, xxvii, xxviii
Birmingham Ethnic Education and Advisory Service, xxvi–xxvii
Birmingham Interfaith Council, xxvii
Birmingham, University of, UK, xiv, xxvii, xxxii, xxxviii, xL, 51
Boal, Barbara M., xx–xxi
Boston bombing, 79
Bosworth, Charles Edmund, xxxvii
Brick Lane. London, xxix
British Council of Churches/Council of Churches for Britain and Ireland, xiii, xxviii–xxxii, xxxvii
Buddhism, xv, xxxiv

GENERAL INDEX

Calvin, John, xxxv–xxxvi
Cambridge University Interfaith Programme, 80, 104
Caner, Emir Fethi and Mehmet Caner, 2, 8
Carey, William, xxiv
Catholic Bishops Conference of England and Wales, xxvii, xxix
Centre for the Study of Islam and Christian-Muslim Relations, Sellly Oak, Birmingham, UK, xiv, xviii, xxx, xxix, xxxi, 1, 27, 32, 46, 47, 74, 76, 84
Centre for the Study of Judaism and Jewish-Christian Relations, Cambridge, UK, xxxviii
Chakrvarti, P. C (David),xxvi
Cheney, Richard (Dick) Bruce, 89
Chittagong, xvii, 31
Christian Witness in a Multi-Religious World: Recommendations, 80–81
Christian-Muslim Relations: a bibliographical history project, xL, 56
Church of England, xxix, 13
Clinton Avenue UMC, Kingston, NY, xxxix, 103
Coffey, David, 79–80
College of Christian Theology, Bangladesh, xxiii
Committee for Relations with People of Other Faiths, xxviii–xxx–ii, xxxiv
Consultation on the Church and the Jewish People, WCC, xxxviii
Contextualization spectrum C1-C6, 12–13
Corbett, Rosemary R., 99
Cordoba, martyrs of, 8
Council of Christian and Jews, UK, xxix, xxxiii
Council on American-Islamic Relations, 77, 96
Cracknell, Kenneth, xxviii, xxx
Cragg, Bishop Kenneth R., xix, 4xx, xxviii, 1, 2, 4, 20–21, 38, 54, 60, 62–65, 68

Deoband Madrasa, India, 29, 30
Dhaka, xvii, xxi, 11, 27
Different Books, Common Word, 79, 102–3
Discernment, xxix, xxx, xxxviii
Document on Human Fraternity, 81, 95

Eaton, Richard M., 31
Egypt, xiii, 61, 62, 88
Elizabeth II, Queen, xxix
Ershad, Hussain Muhammad, 30
Esack, Farid, xxx, xxxvi, 19, 22, 48, 52–55
Esposito, John L., 31, 85, 95
Evangelical Lutheran Church in America, 78

Falwell, Jerry, 8
fanā, 33
fatwā, 88–89
FBI, 96, 100, 101
Fiddes, Paul, 80
Fiqh, 51
First Gulf War, xxix, 86
Ford, David, 104
Fordhouses Baptist Church, Wolverhampton, UK, xv
Forward, Martin, xxx
Francis of Assisi, 8, 23, 42
Francis, Pope, 81, 95
Fuller Theological Seminary, Pasadena, CA, xxiii, 11

Gabriel, angel, 4, 5, 49–50
Gairdner, William Temple, 64
Gallup, 94–95
Gandhi, Mohandas K. xxxi, xxxvii, 23
Georgia, Republic of, 79
Al-Ghazālī, 27, 34, 43
Gibbon, Edward, 14
Goddard, Hugh, xxx
Goodwin, Stephen, xvi
Gospel of Barnabas, 56
Gospel of Judas, 66
Gospel of Thomas, 67
Gospels, non-canonical, 54
Green, Todd, 101

118

GENERAL INDEX

Ground Zero mosque controversy, 98–99
Guidelines (WCC), vii, xxx
Guidelines (BCC), xxx
Guidelines (Vatican), 74–75

ḥadīth, 22, 51,53, 55=56
Haines, Byron, 75
Hajj, 29, 30
Al-Ḥallājj, 33–34
Hartford Seminary, CT, xxxvii, 75–76, 105
Helwys, Thomas, 79
Henry Martyn Institute, Hyderabad, India, xvii, xx, xxxviii
Hick, John, xxxi–xxxii, xxxv, xxxvii, 38, 40–41, 58
Highgate Baptist Church, Birmingham, UK, xxvii, xxxiii–xxxiv
ḥijāb, 101–102
Hijra (622 CE) 17, 62
Hinduism, xv
Hogg, Alfred George, xxxi
Huguenots, xxix, xxxix
ḥulūl (divine indwelling), 26, 32–35
Huntington, Samuel P., 85, 89
Hussain, Saddam, 89
Hussein, M. Kamel, 64–65

Ibn ʿArabī, 34
Ibn Hazm, 56
Ibn Taymiyya, 19,-20, 32
Ilyas, Muḥammad. 30
India, xv–xvi, xx, xxxviii, 8, 10, 30, 61, 66,
Indonesia, xiii, xvii, 91
ʾInjīl, 49, 56
Interfaith Network, UK, xxix
International Interfaith Centre, Oxford, xxxi
Iqbal, Muhammad, 72
Iran hostage crisis, xxiv, 84, 86
Iraq,, xxix, 84, 87, 89, 93
Islamic Circle of North America, 77, 93
Islamic Foundation, Leicester, UK, xix
Islamic Society of North America, 75, 76, 93
Islamic State in Iraq and Syria, 87–88
Islamophobia, 77, 83–87, 102

Israel, xxv, 18, 70, 84, 89
Issues in Christian-Muslim Relations (WCC), xxx, 20, 74

Jamaat-e-Islam, 30
Jesus/ ʿĪsā, xiv, xviii, xvii, xix, xxiv, xxxi–xxxiv .xxxvi, xl, 1–4, 7–8, 11–15, 18–25, 26–29, 31–32, 35–45, 49–50, 53–54, 56–59, 60–72, 76, 78, 107
  Crucifixion of, xix, xL, 12, 40, 53, 55, 56, 60–72
Jihad, 88. 98, 100
Johar, Karan, 96, 99
John of Damascus, 6
Johnson, Elizabeth A., 43, 60, 68–71
Jones, Lewis Bevan, xix, xx, xxii–xxiii, xxv, xxxvi, 10–11, 14, 21–22, 27–28, 35–39, 41–44, 55–57, 62,

Kabbani, Rana, 47, 87–88
Karāmāt, 33
Karamustafa, Ahmet T., 32, 35
Keeler, Cardinal William H., 75
Kennedy, John F., 93
Kerr, David, xvi–xviii, xxv, xxxvii, 1–2, 4, 15–16–19, 21–22, 24, 46, 74
Kerry, John Forbes, 78
Khan, Daisy, 93–94
Khan, Muhammad Yakub, 11
Khan, Sir Sayyid Ahmed, 57
Khatami, Seyyed Mohammad, 85
Khodr, Bishop George, 15–16
Khomeini, Ayotollah Ruholla, 88
Khulna, xxii
King, Peter, 94
Kingston Interfaith Council, NY, xxxix, 103
Kirkwood, Baron Archy of Kirkhope, xxx
Kissinger, Henry, 87
Knysh, Alexander D., 34
Kraemer, Hendrik, xxxi
Kronemer, Alexander, 93
Ku Klux Klan, 93
Kyrgyzstan, 91

Lamb, Christopher, xxx

GENERAL INDEX

Lambton, Nancy, xxx
Latourette, Kenneth Scott, xxiii
Lebanon, 19, 79
Lewis, Bernard, 89–90
Liberation theology, xv, xviii, 19, 52–53
Life (circa 850 CE, Spain), 5–6
Libya, 1, 87
Al-Mahdī, Caliph, 15

Malaysia, xiii, xvi
Mali, 91
Manchester, University of, UK, xv, 39, 55
Mandela, Nelson, 52
Marshall, David, 64
Mary (mother of Jesus), 5, 20, 29, 36, 39, 57–58, 63
Matar, Nabil, 13, 16
McGravan, Donald A., xiii, xxxi
Mecca, 5, 14, 17, 30, 48, 50, 71
Medina, 6, 17, 48, 71
Medley, A. Roy, 79
Methodist Church of Great Britain, xvii, xxix, xxx
Michel, Tom F., 20, 32
Mingana, Alphonse, xiv, 15, 18, 51
Mogahed, Dalia, 95
Morocco, xiii, 8
Moses, 4, 24, 62
Muḥammad, Prophet, xL, 1–25, 26, 32–34, 36–42, 43, 45–50, 54, 56–59, 61–62, 65, 72, 76, 93, 106
Muhammad, Imam W.D., 75
Muhammad: The Legacy of a Prophet, 93–94
Muir, Sir William, 7, 9–10, 14, 17, 45
Muslim Background Believers, 12
Muslim Brotherhood, 84
Muslim Public Affairs Council, USA, 89
Muslim Students' Association, 29
Muslim-nuanced Bengali/Musulman Bangla, xxii, 35
My Name is Khan, 86, 96, 99–102

Nation Council for the Lay Associations, xxviii
National Council of the Churches of Christ USA, xiii, 75–77, 78, 83, 93

Christian Unity Gathering, 83
Convening Table on Interreligious Relations, xiii, 76
National Muslim-Christian Initiative (USA), xxvi, 76–77
New York Times, 91, 97
Newbigin, Lesslie, xvii, xxvii, xxxii–xxxiv, xxxvi
Nicholson, Raymond A., 32–34
Nickel, Gordon, 56
Noah, 57
Northern Baptist College, Manchester, UK, xv, xvii
Nostra Aetate, 73

Obama, Barack H., 93
Oklahoma City bombing, 102
Oriental Institute, Barisal, Bangladesh, xxi
Oxford, University of, xxxviii

Padwick, Constance, 23
Palestinian National Territory/Occupied Territories, xiii, xxv
Parham, Robert, 102
Parrinder, Geoffrey, 26–8, 66
Parshall, Phil, 11–12, 16
Paul of Antioch, 17, 19–20, 32
Pew Research, 81–82, 96
Pipes, Daniel, 89
Pīrs, 30–37,
Pluralism Summit, xxxi–xxxii

Al-Qaeda, 86–97, 90–100
Qur'ān, xviii, xix, xx, xxiv, xxxvii, xL, 18, 19, 24, 27, 28, 32, 36, 41, 45–59, 62, 63–66, 68, 71–72, 77, 80, 88, 94, 98, 102. 106–107

Rābiʿa. 32, 36, 42
Race, Alan, xxxi
Rahner, Karl, xxxi, xxxiv
Ramsey, Charles M., 57
Rangpur, xxiii
Rauschenbusch, Walter, xviii
Risālat al-Kindī, 6–7
Robinson, Neal, xxx

GENERAL INDEX

Rocket, the, xxi–xxii
Roy, Asim, 30
Rūmī, Jalāl ad-Dīn Muhammad, 34
Runnymede Trust, UK, 84
Rushdie, Salman, xxix, 86, 88–89. 98
Russel, Ultan, xxvi, xxviii

el Saadawi, Nawal, 86
Said, Edward, xxviii, 87
Sarder, Ziauddin, 90–91
Sarker, Rekha, xxii, xxviii
Sarker, Roji, xxv
Al-Sarraj, Abu Nasr, 32–33
Sarwar, Muhanmad, 47–48
Saudi Arabia, xxviii, 77, 95
Schiffer, James, xxxix
Schleiermacher, Friedrich D.E., 39
Schuller, Robert, 78
Scriptural Reasoning. 59, 80. 103–105
Senegal, 91
September 11, 2001 (9/11), vii, 48, 77, 81, 86, 91, 93–102. 105
Shairani, Mahmud Khan, 13
Sharīāh, 89
Shoulder to Shoulder Campaign. 91, 102
Sicard, Sigvard von
Siddiqui. Ataulluah, xxx
Ṣifāh, 39, 53
Singh, David Emmanuel, xL, 60
Slomp, Jan, xxvii
Smith, Reginald Bosworth, 16–17. 90
Smith, Wilfred Cantwell, xx, xxxviii
Song of Roland, 6
Soueif, Ahdaf, 88
Southern Baptist Convention, xxxii, 8
Southern Poverty Law Center. 96
Speight, R. Marston, 75
Spencer, Robert, 91
Sprenger, Aloys, 13
Spurgeon, Charles Haddon, xxxv
St. Andrew's Hall, Selly Oak. UK, xiv
State University of New York at New Paltz, xxxix, 29, 84, 96
Stendal, Bishop Krister, 101–102
Stubbe, Henry, 13–14, 16
Submission: a novel, 96–99, 101–102
Ṣūfīsm, xxi, 30–31, 35, 99

Syeed, Sayyid M., 77–78
Systematic theology, xiii

Tablīghī Jamāʿat, xxv, 29–30
Taḥrīf, 56–57
Taizé community, xvii
Taliban, the, 87
Tambaram Missionary Conference, 1938, xxxi
Taqwā (God-consciousness), 28, 37
Taylor, Michael H., xv, xxxvi
Teilhard de Chardin, Pierre, 72
Thatcher, Margaret, 90
Theological Education by Extension, xxiii, xxxviii
Thomas, David, xxx, xL, 20, 51
Thompson, Bishop Jim, xxiv
Timothy II, Patriarch, 15–16, 18
Tisdall, William St-Clair, 10, 12, 55
Toporov, Brandon, 48
Travis, John, 12
Trinity, xix, xxiv, xxxvi, 12–15, 21, 26–29, 37–40, 45, 53, 57–59, 62–63
Troll, Christian, xxxvii
Trump, Donald, 87, 93, 97
Turkey, xiii, 91
Tutu, Desmond, xxvii

Uddin, Sufia M., 30
Union for Reform Judaism, 77
Unitarian, xvii, 12, 14, 33
United Church of Christ, 76
United Nations, 75, 85
United Nations Conference on population, 75
United Reformed Church, xiv, xvii, xxix
United States Conference of Catholic Bishops, 74–75, 78
University of Cambridge interfaith Programme, 80, 104
US Council of Muslim Organizations, 77
USS Cole, 86
ʿUthmān, caliph, 51

Vatican, the, xxxi, xL,73–74, 80–81,
Vaughin, Cliff, 102
Vines, Jerry, 8

GENERAL INDEX

Waldman, Amy, 96–98
Walī, 32, 34, 36, 38
West Midlands Baptist Association, xxvii
Westminster College, Oxford, xxxi, xxxviii
Whitechapel Methodist Mission, xxviii–xxiv
Who Speaks for Islam?, 95
WISE, 94
Woking Mosque, London, 11
Wolfe, Michael, 93
World Congress of Faiths, xxiv
World Council of Churches, xiii, xxx, xxxii, xxxviii, xL, 20, 73–74, 80–81
World Council of Churches Dialogue Sub-Unit, xxx
World Evangelical Alliance, 80–81
World Trade Center bombing, 75

Young, Frances, xxxviii

Zaehner, Robert Charles, 66
Zayd-Zaynab affair, 5, 6, 8
Zaytuna College, Berkeley, CA, 79
Zwemer, Samuel M., 43, 61–62

Scripture Index

OLD TESTAMENT

Genesis
1: 25	57
2:18–29	57
7: 2	57
7: 8–9	57

Exodus
15: 3	57
15: 33	57

NEW TESTAMENT

Matthew
1: 16	57
4: 8	58
5: 48	24
24: 24	12

Luke
3: 23	57
4: 18–20	xxxiii
6: 46	107
3: 30	44

4: 11	58
10: 16	107
14: 16	15
16: 13	23

Ephesians
4: 11	24

Philppians
4: 8	25

QUR'ĀN

2: 148	106
4: 156	63
4: 157	61
4.171	57
5: 38	106
16: 103	6
29: 46	xxiv, 29
33: 37	5
33: 56	24
68: 1–3	6
112–3	28

www.ingramcontent.com/pod-product-compliance
Lightning Source LLC
Chambersburg PA
CBHW071506150426
43191CB00009B/1432